L S D
My Problem Child

Reflections on Sacred Drugs,
Mysticism, and Science

Albert Hofmann, Ph.D.

PUBLISHED BY

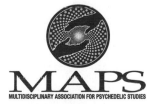

MAPS
MULTIDISCIPLINARY ASSOCIATION FOR PSYCHEDELIC STUDIES

*100% of the profits from the sale
of this book will be devoted to
psychedelic psychotherapy research.*

LSD: My Problem Child
ISBN 978-0-9798622-2-9 (paperback)
Copyright 2009, 1979, 1983, 2005 by Albert Hofmann, Ph.D.
First published in German, 1979 as *LSD: Mein Sorgenkind*

Project Editors: Randolph Hencken, M.A., B.S., 2009 edition
and Brandy Doyle, 2005 edition
English translation by Jonathan Ott, 1983
Cover photo courtesy Rolf Verres
Book & cover design: Mark Plummer
Text set in Figural Book for the Macintosh

Printed in the United States of America by McNaughton & Gunn, Saline, MI

CONTENTS

This new edition of *LSD: My Problem Child*
is funded by a grant to MAPS
from Robert and Erika Barnhart,
in honor of their daughter Phoebe Darling.
May both Phoebe and LSD fulfill their potential
as Wonder Children.

Note From the Publisher of the Fourth English Edition

THIS FOURTH ENGLISH LANGUAGE EDITION of Albert Hofmann's *LSD: My Problem Child* is being published after Albert's recent death. On April 29th, 2008, Albert Hofmann died at the age of 102. Anita Hofmann, Albert's wife for over 72 years, died on December 20, 2007, at the age of 94. Their life-long love affair was an inspiration to all who knew them or knew of them.

Before he died, Albert was fortunate to have the time, the health and the peace of mind to write a summary of his life to be read at his funeral by his two surviving children, Andreas and Beatrix. Albert's family has given us permission to publish a translation of that autobiography as the new introduction to this edition of *LSD: My Problem Child.*

Both Albert and Anita lived long enough to see with their own eyes the renewal of LSD psychotherapy research. Shortly before Anita's death, Swiss psychiatrist Dr. Peter Gasser obtained government approval for his MAPS-sponsored study of LSD-assisted psychotherapy in subjects with anxiety associated with end-of-life issues. Albert spoke about the renewal of LSD psychotherapy research as "the fulfillment of my heart's desire."

Shortly before he died, Albert said that he'd continue to help support the renaissance in LSD psychotherapy research either from "this side or the other side." Through the publication of this book, Albert continues to support the transformation of his "problem child" into a "wonder child."

The first LSD session in the Swiss study took place on Tuesday, May 13, 2008. This session is part of the first controlled, scientific study of the therapeutic potential of LSD in over 36 years. More information about the psychedelic research renaissance can be found at the end of this book in the "About the Publisher" section or online at www.maps.org

Shortly after his 100th birthday, Albert said:

In the future, I hope that LSD provides to the individual a new worldview, which is in harmony with nature and its laws.

I am hopeful about the future evolution of the human species. I am hopeful because I have the impression that more and more human individuals are becoming conscious, and that the creative spirit, which we call "God," speaks to us through his creation—through the endlessness of the starry sky, through the beauty and wonder of the living individuals of the plant, the animal, and the human kingdoms.

We human beings are able to understand this message because we possess the divine gift of consciousness. This connects us to the universal mind and gives us divine creativity. Any means that helps to expand our individual consciousness—by opening up and sharpening our inner and outer eyes, in order to understand the divine universal message—will help humanity to survive. An understanding of the divine message—in its universal language—would bring an end to the war between the religions of the world.

Albert himself took LSD for the last time at age 97.

The Life of Albert Hofmann:
January 11, 1906 to April 29, 2008

By Albert Hofmann, Ph.D.

Translation from German by Elisabeth Riccabona

LOOKING BACK ON MY LIFE, I presume that the constellation of stars—or that whatever could determine one's fate in life—indicated good fortune when I saw the light of day on January 11, 1906 in Baden, Canton of Aargau.

My father, Adolf Hofmann, and my mother Elisabeth, born Schenk, met in Münchenstein, near Basel, where my father worked as a locksmith for one of the subsidiaries of the mechanical engineering group Brown-Boveri. Soon afterwards, he was transferred to the company's headquarters in Baden.

Although my father rapidly progressed to the position of foreman, and then master in the tool-making division, our family had to live a rather modest lifestyle as wages, even for such a position, were low at that time. Together, with my younger brother and my two younger sisters, I lived a childhood which was not always free of worries but on the whole quite a happy one.

My first childhood memory is an image of large red strawberries in the garden where my mother used to carry me around in her arms. Another image I remember: It is night time, many people are standing in the street. They are pointing towards the sky in excitement. There is a comet in the sky. It was the Halley's Comet in 1910.

Another striking memory I have is of the day we moved from Schönau Street to Martinsberg Street. I am standing in front of the house, holding my little brother's hand and looking at the new neighborhood, where rowan berry trees glow golden in the autumn sun.

Between the age of five and ten we lived there, beneath the hill upon which the remains of Stein Castle were standing. On the opposite side of the street was a farmhouse, next to it a blacksmith's shop and a wainwright's. I played with the farmer's kids in the barn and was in the stable when the farmer milked the cows. I was riding along with the farmers on carts, pulled by cows or horses, to the fields where the animals could graze. I rode with them to make hay, and in autumn up to the Allmend which lay high above town. Up there you could often hear the distant roaring of guns sounding from the Alsace; it was at the time of the First World War. I also spent a lot of time at the blacksmith's, watching how the blacksmith shoed the horses and wound the red hot iron hoops onto the wooden cartwheels.

The area surrounding the remains of Stein Castle was a wonderful place for us kids to play. I can still remember hearing my mother calling out from the kitchen window for us kids to come in for lunch or dinner when we had forgotten all about time while playing up in the ruins. The way to school, which led through the old town gate and through alleyways of the old town, always brings forth many fond memories.

It was like the banishment from a child's paradise when we moved away from Martinsberg Street to Dynamo Street, to a hideous apartment building directly across from the factory entrance. We were forced to move due to my father's illness – he was suffering from pulmonary tuberculosis – which had deteriorated, and even the short way from Martinsberg Street to the factory had become too strenuous for him.

Whenever I could, I left the grim and dreary factory quarters and went back up to Martinsberg, into the forest, to the meadows and fields. During these expeditions I experienced the magic and charm of the Jura landscape, which was in constant change with the seasons.

It was there that, during enchanted moments, the wonder of creation revealed itself to me in the beauty of nature, and already then forged my view of the world in its basic features.

After finishing elementary school I had planned to attend high school in order to be granted entry into university. However, considering my father's serious illness, my parents thought I should ensure my own income as quickly as possible, and so it was that they sent me to start a commercial apprenticeship with Brown-Boveri.

After dutifully completing the three year apprenticeship, and obtaining security regarding my future professional life in the form of a diploma, my dream to go to university eventually came true. My dear godfather Hans Kühni, founder of the Kühni machine factory in Allschwil, paid for the tuition fees at the Minerva private school in Zurich. I absorbed the knowledge like a dry sponge and passed the general qualification for university entrance in Latin after only one year.

Fascinated by the mysteries of the subject, I decided to study chemistry at the University of Zurich. As a citizen of Weiningen in the Canton of Zurich I received a scholarship from the university. Living with my parents in Baden with no money for any distractions I immersed myself completely in my studies as my only enjoyment. Professor Paul Karrer, Director for the Department of Chemistry at that time, soon found me a position as an assistant to the professor. At the age of 23 I had already finished my Chemistry studies, after only eight semesters and received my Ph.D.

My father passed away three months before I finished my studies. However, before his death I was still able to show him my employment contract which I had already signed with Sandoz Pharmaceuticals.

In May 1929, I started my professional life, joining the Basel-based Pharmaceutical-Chemical Department of Sandoz Laboratories, whose director was Professor Arthur Stoll. At the laboratories we were studying the properties of medicinal plants, the kind of work that entirely fulfilled my love of plants. I found complete satisfaction in my work when isolating, elucidating the chemical structure, and synthesizing the active substances of medicinal plants. So it was that my whole professional career evolved all around the Sandoz Pharmaceutical Laboratories, starting off as a coworker with Professor Stoll, working my way up to become team leader, and eventually being appointed Director of Research for the Department of Natural Products.

Valuable drugs like Methergine, Dihydergot, and Hydergine derive from substances I produced during my studies. By research and chance I discovered the psychoactive agent, which became known worldwide as LSD. In my book titled, *LSD: My Problem Child*, I illustrated the history of LSD and its relation to the Mexican magic mushrooms. During lecture tours and conference visits I formed lasting friendships, mainly with colleagues from the United States, Mexico and Sweden.

The shining light that guided me through my professional career also accompanied me in my private life. In Anita Guanella I found the partner who gave me great happiness in marriage and in my family.

We met in 1934 while on skiing holidays in Arosa. The first five years of our marriage we lived in Basel on Holee Street. Our two sons, Dieter and Andreas were born there. Several times during the war I had to go to Ticino for a few months to serve in the army.

During a holiday in May 1946, we moved to the countryside, to Oberwiler Street in the municipality of Bottmingen. For the next twenty-seven years we lived there, in our own house with its beautiful garden standing amidst a then still entirely rural area. My family soon grew bigger. We were blessed with two daughters, Gaby and Beatrix.

Only some of the many fond memories I have of that wonderful time, the middle of my life, I shall mention here: Our holidays in the Engadin valley, where Anita felt particularly happy as she originally came from the Canton of Graubünden, the home of her parents. While hiking and mountaineering together we experienced the magic, grandeur and sublime beauty of this high mountain valley. One of the highlights was certainly our ascent to the Bernina peak.

I also very fondly remember the great trips to India, Thailand, and particularly the expedition to indigenous Indian areas in Mexico. These trips were part of my work and Anita used to always accompany me.

Shortly before it was time for me to retire, and after the formerly rural and quiet municipality of Bottmingen had developed into a busy suburb, we decided to move further out into the countryside. In the village of Burg, at the very end of the Leimen valley, we found the ideal place to live. According to the plans and ideas of each family member, we built a house up at Rittimatte. There we lived happily for many years, particularly enjoying the many visits from our children, grandchildren and friends. While Anita found her love and joy in caring for flowers in our garden and house, like she already did in Bottmingen, I spent my time in the silence of my "hermitage," writing literary works, publications and dissertations, partly associated with my former occupation, as well as writing down my personal understandings and thoughts on natural philosophy.

It was also up at Rittimatte that my circle of life closed itself as I found the paradise of my childhood again, the same landscape as on Martinsberg, where I used to be blissful as a boy, the same meadows with the same flowers and the same view into the far distance.

Paracelsus described nature and creation as a "book that was written by God's finger". During my life I was given this exhilarating and entirely comforting experience: The one who understands how to read this book, not only with regards to scientific research but with marveling and loving eyes, will find a deeper, wonderful reality revealing itself–a reality in which we are all secure and united for ever and ever.

Foreword
Stanislav Grof, M.D.

THE USE OF PSYCHEDELIC SUBSTANCES can be traced back for millennia, to the dawn of human history. Since time immemorial, plant materials containing powerful consciousness-expanding compounds have been used in many different parts of the world to induce non-ordinary states of consciousness in various ritual and spiritual contexts. They have played an important role in shamanic practice, aboriginal healing ceremonies, rites of passage, mysteries of death and rebirth, and spiritual traditions. The ancient and native cultures using psychedelic materials held them in great esteem and considered them to be sacraments, "flesh of the gods."

Human groups, which had at their disposal psychedelic plants, took advantage of their entheogenic effects (entheogenic means literally "awakening the divine within") and made them the principal vehicle of their ritual and spiritual life. The preparations made from these plants mediated for these people experiential contact with the archetypal dimensions of reality—deities, mythological realms, power animals, and numinous forces and aspects of nature. Another important area where states induced by psychedelics played a crucial role was diagnosing and healing of various disorders.

Anthropological literature contains many reports indicating that native cultures use psychedelics to cultivate intuition and extrasensory perception for a variety of divinatory, as well as practical purposes, such as finding lost persons and objects, obtaining information about people in remote locations, and for following the movement of the game these people hunted. In addition, psychedelic experiences served as important sources of artistic inspiration, providing ideas for rituals, paintings, sculptures, and songs.

In the history of Chinese medicine, reports about psychedelic substances can be traced back about 3,000 years. The legendary divine potion referred to as *haoma* in the ancient Persian *Zend Avesta* and as *soma* in the Indian Vedas was used by the Indo-Iranian tribes millenia ago. The mystical states of consciousness induced by soma were very likely the principal source of the Vedic and Hindu religion. Preparations from different varieties of hemp have been smoked and ingested under various names— *hashish, charas, bhang, ganja, kif,* and *marijuana*—in Asia, in Africa, and in the Caribbean area for recreation, pleasure, and during religious ceremonies. They represented an important sacrament for such diverse groups as the Indian Brahmans, certain orders of Sufis, ancient Scythians, and the Jamaican Rastafarians.

Ceremonial use of various psychedelic substances also has a long history in Central America. Highly effective mind-altering plants were well known in several Pre-Columbian Indian cultures—among the Aztecs, Mayans, Olmecs, and Mazatecs. The most famous of these are the Mexican cactus peyote (*Anhalonium Lewinii*), the sacred mushroom *teonanacatl* (*Psilocybe mexicana*) and *ololiuhqui*, or morning glory seeds (*Rivea corymbosa*). These materials have been used as sacraments until this day by several Mexican Indian tribes (Huichols, Mazatecs, Cora people, and others) and by the Native American Church.

The famous South American *yajé* or *ayahuasca* is a decoction from a jungle liana (*Banisteriopsis caapi*) with other plant additives. The Amazonian area is also known for a variety of psychedelic snuffs (*Virola callophylla, Piptadenia peregrina*). Preparations from the bark of the shrub iboga (*Tabernanthe iboga*) have been used by African tribes in lower dosage as a stimulant during lion hunts and long canoe trips and in higher doses as a ritual sacrament. The above list represents only a small fraction of psychedelic compounds that have been used over many centuries in various countries of the world. The impact that the experiences encountered in these states had on the spiritual and cultural life of pre-industrial societies has been enormous.

People from our culture, who see the use of psychedelic plants as something that is practiced in exotic and "primitive" cultures and is alien to our own tradition would be very surprised to find out that psychedelic substances very likely profoundly influenced the ancient Greek culture, generally considered the cradle of the European civilization. Many giants of Greek culture, including Plato, Aristotle, Alkibiades, Pindaros, and others were initiates in the Mediterranean mysteries of death and rebirth held in the names of Demeter and Persephone, Dionysus, Attis, Adonis, Orpheus, and others. According to a theory proposed by a research team that included Albert Hofmann himself, the sacred potion *kykeon* administered to thousands of initiates in the Eleusinian mysteries every five years for almost two millennia contained an ergot alkaloid similar to LSD. Psychedelics were also very likely ingredients in the wines used for the Bacchanalia.

The long history of ritual use of psychedelic plants contrasts sharply with a relatively short history of scientific efforts to identify their psychoactive alkaloids and to study their effects. The first psychedelic substance that was synthetized in a chemically pure form and systematically explored under laboratory conditions was mescaline, the active alkaloid from the peyote cactus. Clinical experiments conducted with this substance in the first three decades of the twentieth century focused on the phenomenology of the mescaline experience and its interesting effects on artistic perception and creative expression. Surprisingly, they did not reveal its therapeutic, heuristic, and entheogenic potential. Kurt Beringer, author of the influential book *Der Meskalinrausch* (Mescaline Inebriation) published in 1927, concluded that mescaline induced a toxic psychosis.

After these pioneering clinical experiments with mescaline, very little research was done in this fascinating problem area until Albert Hofmann's 1942 epoch-making serendipitous discovery of the psychedelic properties of LSD-25, or diethylamid of lysergic acid, a substance of extraordinary potency. This new semisynthetic ergot derivative, active in incredibly minute quantities of micrograms or gammas (millionths of a gram) started a revolutionary era of research in psychopharmacology, psychology, psychiatry, and psychotherapy. Because of the incredible promises it held in many different fields of research, this new substance appeared to be Albert Hofmann's "prodigious child."

The discovery of powerful psychedelic effects of miniscule dosages of LSD started what has been called a "golden era of psychopharmacology." During a relatively short period of time, the joint efforts of biochemists, pharmacologists, neurophysiologists, psychiatrists, and psychologists succeeded in laying the foundations of a new scientific discipline that can be referred to as "pharmacology of consciousness." The active substances from several remaining psychedelic plants were chemically identified and prepared in chemically pure form. Following the discovery of the psychedelic effects of LSD-25, Albert Hofmann identified the active principles of the Mexican magic mushrooms (*Psilocybe mexicana*), psilocybin and psilocin, and that of ololiuhqui, or morning glory seeds (*Rivea corymbosa*), which turned out to be lysergic acid amide, closely related to LSD-25.

The armamentarium of psychedelic substances was further enriched by psychoactive derivatives of tryptamine—DMT (dimethyl-tryptamine, DET (diethyl-tryptamine), and DPT (dipropyltryptamine)—synthetized and studied by the Budapest group of chemists, headed by Steven Szara, The active principle from the African shrub *Tabernanthe iboga*, ibogaine, and the pure alkaloid from ayahuasca's main ingredient *Banisteriopsis caapi*, known under the names harmaline, yageine, and telepathine had already been isolated and chemically identified earlier in the twentieth century. In the 1950s, a wide range of psychedelic alkaloids in pure form was available to researchers. It was now possible to study their properties in the laboratory and explore the phenomenology of their clinical effects and their therapeutic potential. The revolution triggered by Albert Hofmann's serendipitous discovery of LSD was underway.

After the publication of the first clinical paper on LSD by Walter A. Stoll in the late 1940s, in which the author described the effects of this extraordinary substance in a group of volunteers and psychiatric patients and mentioned its possible therapeutic potential, Albert Hofmann's "wonder child" became an overnight sensation in the scientific world. Never before in the history of science had a single substance held so much promise in such a wide variety of fields.

For neuropharmacologists and neurophysiologists, the discovery of LSD meant the beginning of a golden era of research that could solve many puzzles concerning neuroreceptors, synaptic transmitters, chemical antagonisms, the role of serotonin in the brain, and the intricate biochemical interactions underlying cerebral processes.

Experimental psychiatrists saw LSD as a unique means for creating a laboratory model for naturally occurring functional, or endogenous, psychoses. They hoped that the "experimental psychosis," induced by miniscule dosages of this substance, could provide unparalleled insights into the nature of these mysterious disorders and open new avenues for their treatment. It was suddenly conceivable that the brain or other parts of the body could under certain circumstances produce small quantities of a substance with similar effects as LSD. This meant that disorders like schizophrenia would not be mental diseases, but metabolic aberrations that could be counteracted by specific chemical intervention. The promise of this research was nothing less that the fulfillment of the dream of biologically oriented clinicians, the Holy Grail of psychiatry – a test-tube cure for schizophrenia.

LSD was also highly recommended as an extraordinary unconventional teaching device that would make it possible for clinical psychiatrists, psychologists, medical students, and nurses to spend a few hours in the world of their patients and as a result of it to understand them better, be able to communicate with them more effectively, and improve their ability to help them. Thousands of mental health professionals took advantage of this unique opportunity. These experiments brought surprising and astonishing results. They not only provided deep insights into the world of psychiatric patients, but also revolutionized the understanding of the nature and dimensions of the human psyche.

Many found that the current model, limiting the psyche to postnatal biography and the Freudian individual unconscious, was superficial and inadequate. The new map of the psyche that emerged out of this research added two large transbiographical domains – the perinatal level, closely related to the memory of biological birth, and the transpersonal level, harboring the historical and archetypal domains of the collective unconscious as envisioned by C. C. Jung. Early experiments with LSD showed that the roots of emotional and psychosomatic disorders were not limited to traumatic memories from childhood and infancy, as traditional psychiatrists assumed, but reached much deeper into the psyche, into the perinatal and transpersonal regions.

Reports from psychedelic psychotherapists revealed LSD's unique potential as a powerful tool offering the possibility of deepening and accelerating the psychotherapeutic process. Using LSD as a catalyst, it became possible to extend the range of applicability of psychotherapy to categories of patients that previously had been difficult to reach – sexual deviants, alcoholics, narcotic drug addicts, and criminal recidivists.

Particularly valuable and promising were the early efforts to use
LSD psychotherapy in the work with terminal cancer patients.
Research on this population showed that LSD was able to relieve
severe pain, often even in those patients who had not responded
to medication with narcotics. In a large percentage of these
patients, it was also possible to ease or even eliminate difficult
emotional and psychosomatic symptoms, such as depression,
general tension, and insomnia, alleviate the fear of death, increase
the quality of their life during the remaining days, and positively
transform the experience of dying.

For historians and critics of art, the LSD experiments
provided extraordinary new insights into the psychology and
psychopathology of art, particularly various modern movements,
such as abstractionism, cubism, surrealism, fantastic realism,
and into paintings and sculptures of various native, so-called
"primitive" cultures. For professional painters, who participated
in LSD research, the psychedelic session often marked a radical
change in their artistic expression. Their imagination became
much richer, their colors more vivid, and their style considerably
freer. They could also often reach into deep recesses of their
unconscious psyche and tap archetypal sources of inspiration.
On occasion, people who had never painted before were able to
produce extraordinary pieces of art.

LSD experimentation brought also fascinating observations,
which were of great interest to spiritual teachers and scholars
of comparative religion. The mystical experiences frequently
observed in LSD sessions offered a radically new understanding
of a wide variety of phenomena from the world of religion,
including shamanism, the rites of passage, the ancient mysteries
of death and rebirth, the Eastern spiritual philosophies, and the
mystical traditions of the world. The fact that LSD and other
psychedelic substances were able to trigger a broad range of
spiritual experiences became the subject of heated scientific
discussions. They revolved around the fascinating problem

concerning the nature and value of this "instant" or "chemical" mysticism,"

LSD research seemed to be well on its way to fulfill all the above promises and expectations when it was suddenly interrupted by the unsupervised mass experimentation of the young generation. In the infamous Harvard affair, Timothy Leary, Richard Alpert and Ralph Metzner left the university (Leary and Alpert leaving teaching posts, and Metzner losing a fellowship) after their overeager proselytizing of LSD and psilocybin. The ensuing repressive measures of administrative, legal, and political nature had very little effect on street use of LSD and other psychedelics, but they drastically terminated legitimate clinical research. However, while the problems associated with this development were blown out of proportion by sensation-hunting journalists, this was not the only reason why LSD and other psychedelics were rejected by the Euro-American culture. An important contributing factor was also the attitude of technological societies toward non-ordinary states of consciousness.

As I mentioned earlier, all ancient and pre-industrial societies held these states in high esteem, whether they were induced by psychedelic plants or some of the many powerful non-drug "technologies of the sacred" – fasting, sleep deprivation, social and sensory isolation, dancing, chanting, music, drumming, or physical pain. Members of these social groups had the opportunity to repeatedly experience non-ordinary states of consciousness during their lives in a variety of sacred and secular contexts. By comparison, the industrial civilizations have pathologized non-ordinary states, developed effective means of suppressing them when they occur spontaneously, and have rejected or even outlawed the contexts and tools that can facilitate them. Because of the resulting naiveté and ignorance concerning non-ordinary states, Western culture was unprepared to accept and incorporate the extraordinary mind-altering properties and power of LSD and other psychedelics.

The sudden invasion of the Dionysian element from the depths of the unconscious and the heights of the superconscious was too threatening for the Puritanical values of Euro-American society. In addition, the irrational and transrational nature of psychedelic experiences seriously challenged the very foundations of the materialistic worldview of Western science. The existence and nature of these experiences could not be explained in the context of mainstream theories and seriously undermined the metaphysical assumptions concerning priority of matter over consciousness on which Western culture is built. It also threatened the leading myth of the industrial world by showing that true fulfillment does not come from achievement of material goals but from a profound mystical experience.

It was not just the culture at large that was unprepared for the psychedelic experience; it was also the helping profession. For most psychiatrists and psychologists, psychotherapy meant disciplined face to-face discussions or free-associating on the couch. The intense emotions and dramatic physical manifestations in psychedelic sessions appeared to them to be too close to what they were used to associate with psychopathology. It was hard for them to imagine that such states could be healing and transformative. As a result, they did not trust the reports about the extraordinary power of psychedelic psychotherapy coming from those colleagues who had enough courage to take the chances and do psychedelic therapy, or from their clients.

To complicate the situation even further, many of the phenomena occurring in psychedelic sessions could not be understood within the context of theories dominating academic thinking. The possibility of reliving birth or episodes from embryonic life, obtaining accurate information about world history and mythology from the collective unconscious, experiencing archetypal realities and karmic memories, or perceiving remote events in out-of-body states, were simply too fantastic to be believable for an average professional. Yet those of us who had the chance to work with LSD and were willing to radically change our theoretical understanding of the psyche and practical strategy of therapy were able to see and appreciate the enormous potential of psychedelics, both as therapeutic tools and as substances of extraordinary heuristic value.

In one of my early books, I suggested that the potential significance of LSD and other psychedelics for psychiatry and psychology was comparable to the value the microscope has for biology and medicine or the telescope has for astronomy. My later experience with psychedelics only confirmed this initial impression. These substances function as unspecific amplifiers that increase the cathexis (energetic charge) associated with the deep unconscious contents of the psyche and make them available for conscious processing. This unique property of psychedelics makes it possible to study psychological undercurrents that govern our experiences and behaviors to a depth that cannot be matched by any other method and tool available in modern mainstream psychiatry and psychology. In addition, it offers unique opportunities for healing of emotional and psychosomatic disorders, for positive personality transformation, and consciousness evolution.

Naturally, the tools of this power carry with them greater risks than more conservative and far less effective tools currently accepted and used by mainstream psychiatry, such as verbal psychotherapy or tranquillizing medication. Responsible clinical research has shown that these risks can be minimized by responsible use and careful control of the set and setting. However, legislators responding to unsupervised mass use of psychedelics did not get their information from scientific publications, but from the stories of sensation-hunting journalists. The legal and administrative sanctions against psychedelics did not deter lay experimentation, but they terminated all legitimate scientific research of these substances. By an unfortunate combination of circumstances, Albert Hofmann's wonder child became a "problem child."

For those of us who had the privilege to explore and experience the extraordinary potential of psychedelics, this was a tragic loss for psychiatry, psychology, and psychotherapy. We felt that these unfortunate developments wasted what was probably the single most important opportunity in the history of these disciplines. Had it been possible to avoid the unnecessary mass hysteria and continue responsible research of psychedelics, they could have radically transformed the theory and practice of psychiatry. This research would have brought a new understanding of the psyche and of consciousness that could become an integral part of a comprehensive new scientific paradigm of the twenty-first century.

LSD researchers responded in different ways to the legal and political sanctions against psychedelics. Some of them grudgingly accepted them and reluctantly returned to mainstream therapeutic practices, which now seemed to them boring and painfully ineffective. A few of us attempted to develop non-drug methods for inducing non-ordinary states of consciousness with the experiential spectrum and healing potential comparable to psychedelics. There were also those who saw the extraordinary benefits of LSD psychotherapy and decided not to sacrifice the wellbeing of their clients to irrational and scientifically unsubstantiated legislation, and continued their work in secret. In addition to the therapeutic value of psychedelics, many of these professionals were also aware of the entheogenic potential of these substances. For this reason, they understood their work with LSD to be not only therapeutic practice, but also religious activity in the best sense of the word. From this perspective, the legal sanctions against psychedelics appeared to be not only unfounded and misguided, but represented a serious infringement of religious freedom guaranteed by the American Constitution.

At present, when more than three decades elapsed since official

LSD research was effectively terminated, I can attempt to evaluate the past history of this substance and glimpse into its future. After having personally conducted over the last fifty years more than four thousand psychedelic sessions, I have developed great awe and respect for these substances and their enormous positive, as well as negative potential. They are powerful tools and like any tool they can be used skillfully, ineptly, or destructively. The result will be critically dependent on the set and setting.

The question whether LSD is a phenomenal medicine or a devil's drug makes as little sense as a similar question asked about the positive or negative potential of a knife. Naturally, we will get a very different report from a surgeon who bases his or her judgment on successful operations and from the police chief who investigates murders committed with knives in back alleys of New York City. It would also make little sense to judge the usefulness and dangers of a knife by watching children who play with it without adequate maturity and skill. Similarly, the image of LSD will vary whether we focus on the results of responsible clinical or spiritual use, naive and careless mass self-experimentation of the young generation, or deliberately destructive experiments of the Army or the CIA.

Until it is clearly understood that the results of the administration of psychedelics are critically influenced by the factors of set and setting, there is no hope for rational decisions in regard to psychedelic drug policies. I firmly believe that psychedelics can be used in such a way that the benefits far outweigh the risks. This has been amply proven by millenia of safe ritual and spiritual use of psychedelics by generations of shamans, individual healers, and entire aboriginal cultures. However, the Western industrial civilization has so far abused nearly all its discoveries and there is not much hope that psychedelics will make an exception, unless we rise as a group to a higher level of consciousness and emotional maturity.

Whether or not psychedelics will return into psychiatry and

will again become part of the therapeutic armamentarium is a complex problem and its solution will probably be determined not only by the results of scientific research, but also by a variety of political, legal, economic, and mass-psychological factors. However, I believe that Western society is at present much better equipped to accept and assimilate psychedelics than it was in the 1950s. At the time when psychiatrists and psychologists started to experiment with LSD, psychotherapy was limited to verbal exchanges between therapist and clients. Intense emotions and active behavior were referred to as "acting-out" and were seen as violations of basic therapeutic rules. Psychedelic sessions were on the other side of the spectrum, evoking dramatic emotions, psychomotor excitement, and vivid perceptual changes. They thus seemed to be more like states that psychiatrists considered pathological and tried to suppress by all means than conditions to which one would attribute therapeutic potential. This was reflected in the terms "hallucinogens," "delirogens," "psychotomimetics," and "experimental psychoses," used initially for psychedelics and the states induced by them. In any case, psychedelic sessions more resembled scenes from anthropological movies about healing rituals of "primitive" cultures and other ceremonies than those expected in a psychoanalyst's office.

In addition, many of the experiences and observations from psychedelic sessions seemed to seriously challenge the image of the human psyche and of the universe developed by Newtonian-Cartesian science and considered to be accurate and definitive descriptions of "objective reality." Psychedelic subjects reported experiential identification with other people, animals, and various aspects of nature, during which they gained access to new information about areas about which they previously had no intellectual knowledge. The same was true about experiential excursions into the lives of their human and animal ancestors, as well as racial, collective, and karmic memories.

On occasion, this new information was drawn from

experiences involving reliving biological birth and memories of prenatal life, encounters with archetypal beings, and visits mythological realms of different cultures of the world. In out-of-body experiences, experimental subjects were able to witness and accurately describe remote events occurring in locations that were outside of the range of their senses. None of these happenings were considered possible in the context of traditional materialistic science, and yet, in psychedelic sessions, they were observed frequently. This naturally caused deep conceptual turmoil and confusion in the minds of conventionally trained experimenters. Under these circumstances, many professionals chose to stay away from this area to preserve their scientific world-view and to protect their common sense and sanity.

The last three decades have brought many revolutionary changes that have profoundly influenced the climate in the world of psychotherapy. Humanistic and transpersonal psychologies have developed powerful experiential techniques that emphasize deep regression, direct expression of intense emotions, and bodywork leading to release of physical energies. Among these new approaches to self-exploration are Gestalt practice, bioenergetics and other neo-Reichian methods, primal therapy, rebirthing, and holotropic breathwork. The inner experiences and outer manifestations, as well as therapeutic strategies, in these therapies bear a great similarity to those observed in psychedelic sessions. These non-drug therapeutic strategies involve a similar spectrum of experiences, as well as comparable conceptual challenges. As a result, for therapists practicing along these lines, the introduction of psychedelics would represent the next logical step rather than dramatic change in their practice.

The culture at large shows encouraging signs as well. Grassroots movements around birth and death, for example, reveal a growing discontent with the sanitization of powerful experiences. Today, midwives can be state certified and home births are increasingly popular, whereas in the 1950s these were considered backwards or primitive. People can choose to die at home, thanks to the hospice movement, instead of in sterile hospital settings. Previously eccentric healing techniques, like massage and acupuncture, are widely accepted, even by health insurance plans. Eastern spiritual practices have moved to the mainstream of Western culture, with meditation centers and yoga schools to be found in every major city. Increasingly, the authority of traditional medical science, with its firm separation between mind and body, is becoming suspect, and people are seeking more holistic alternatives. These shifts may signal that society is more ready for psychedelics today.

Moreover, the Newtonian-Cartesian thinking in science, which in the 1960s enjoyed great authority and popularity, has been progressively undermined by astonishing developments in a variety of disciplines. This has happened to such an extent that an increasing number of scientists feel an urgent need for an entirely different world-view, a new scientific paradigm. Salient examples of this development are philosophical implications of quantum-relativistic physics, David Bohm's theory of holomovement, Karl Pribram's holographic theory of the brain, Ilya Prigogine's theory of dissipative structures, Rupert Sheldrake's theory of morphogenetic fields, Gregory Bateson's brilliant synthesis of systems and information theory, cybernetics, anthropology, and psychology, and particularly Ervin Laszlo's concept of the akashic field, his connectivity hypothesis, and his "integral theory of everything." It is very encouraging to see that all these new developments that are in irreconcilable conflict with traditional science seem to be compatible with the findings of psychedelic research and with transpersonal psychology.

Even more encouraging than the changes in the general scientific climate is the fact that, in a few cases, researchers of the younger generation in the United States and abroad have in recent years been able to obtain official permission to start programs of psychedelic therapy, involving LSD, psilocybin, dimethyltryptamine (DMT), methylene-dioxy-methamphetamine (MDMA), and ketamine. I hope that this is the beginning of a renaissance of interest in psychedelic research that will eventually return these extraordinary tools into the hands of responsible therapists. I personally believe that in the future LSD will be seen as one of the most influential discoveries of the twentieth century and that Albert Hofmann's "problem child" will again be seen – as it should have been seen all along – as a "wonder child" that had to grow up in a dysfunctional society.

I would like to end this foreword on a personal note. Writing it gives me the opportunity to express my profound gratitude to Albert Hofmann for everything that his discovery brought into my personal and professional life and the lives of countless others who used his gift responsibly and with respect that this extraordinary tool deserves. I have had the privilege to know Albert personally and meet him repeatedly on various occasions. Over the years, I have developed great affection and deep admiration for him, not only as an outstanding scientist, but also as an extraordinary human being. After what will soon be a century of a full, blessed, and productive life, he radiates amazing vitality, curiosity, and love for all creation.

I had another opportunity to meet Albert during my recent visit in Switzerland, where I was teaching an advanced training module on holotropic breathwork entitled Fantastic Art. It was held in the H. R. Giger Museum in Gruyère and Albert came as a guest of honor. After we had lunch and enjoyed a guided tour through the museum, during which he braved three floors of steep stairs, he sat down with our group for a discussion which turned into his passionate apotheosis of the beauty and mystery of creation. He spoke about the miraculous chemistry that gives rise to the pigments responsible for the colors of flowers and butterfly wings, about the gratitude he felt for being alive and participating in consciousness, and about the need to embrace creation in its totality, including its shadow side, because without

Stanislav Grof, with Albert Hofmann and H. R. Giger
at The H. R. Giger Museum in Gruyere, Switzerland,
October 2005 Photograph by Wolfgang Holz.

polarity the universe we live in could not have been created.

When he left, we all felt that we just had attended a darshan
with a spiritual teacher. It was clear that Albert had joined
the group of great scientists—like Albert Einstein and Isaac
Newton—for whom rigorous pursuit of their discipline brought
the recognition of the miraculous divine order underlying the
world of matter and the natural phenomena. I would like to use
this opportunity to wish him all the best for his forthcoming
auspicious hundredth anniversary and hope that we will enjoy
his presence in the world for many more years.

STANISLAV GROF
Mill Valley, California,
October 2005.

Preface to the new edition

Albert Hofmann

AT THE END OF THE LAST INTRODUCTION, written over 30 years ago, I expressed my hope that the problem child LSD might become a miracle child, if one could learn how to make use of its extraordinary psychic effects.

BUT LSD IS STILL A PROBLEM CHILD.

After LSD had been used nearly exclusively in medicine and biological research for decades, it entered the drug scene in the sixties. It was for a time the number one drug in mass consumption, especially in the U.S., with all the problems associated with this. Following this, the health authorities imposed a draconian prohibition, which also banned the use of LSD and related substances in medical practice, psychiatry and psychology. This ban is still in place today. Although this is how the medical use of LSD came to a halt, the private use continues, with all the dangers and difficulties of a drug forced into illegality.

Efforts from psychiatrists petitioning health authorities to again release LSD for medical application have so far been unsuccessful. This is difficult to understand, because the documented experiences show that use in medical settings is safe, and that LSD can be beneficial as a supplemental medication in psychiatry.

The ban also looks questionable in another light, after components similar to LSD were found in sacred Mexican drugs that have been used medicinally for thousands of years. There is a wealth of experience with these substances that should be taken into account.

It is no accident that it was LSD which brought these Mexican drugs into my laboratory for chemical analysis. It was the similarity in the psychological effects between these sacred plants and LSD which lead the anthropologists and botanists who had explored their use by the Mazatec in the mountains of southern Mexico to hand the chemical analysis to the same laboratory where LSD was discovered. The analysis gave the surprising result that the chemical structure of the components extracted from these plants was related closely to the structure of LSD.

This resulted in the important finding that LSD belongs chemically, as well as in its psychological effects, to this group of sacred Mexican drugs. Thus the adventure of the discovery of LSD found a surprising continuation 15 years later, in the exciting discovery of ancient sacred drugs—the account of which covers a big part of this book.

[Publisher's note: The struggle to return LSD to legitimacy continues, and it is with this hope that MAPS (the Multidisciplinary Association for Psychedelic Studies) has re-published Dr. Hofmann's book, on the occasion of his 100th birthday. See the "About the Publisher" section at the end of this book for more information and ways to get involved.]

Translator's Preface

NUMEROUS ACCOUNTS of the discovery of LSD have been published in English; none, unfortunately, have been completely accurate. Here, at last, the father of LSD details the history of his "problem child" and his long and fruitful career as a research chemist. In a real sense, this book is the inside story of the birth of the Psychedelic Age, and it cannot be denied that we have here a highly candid and personal insight into one of the most important scientific discoveries of our time, the significance of which has yet to dawn on mankind.

Surpassing its historical value is the immense philosophical import of this work. Never before has a chemist, an expert in the most materialistic of the sciences, advanced a *Weltanschauung* of such a mystical and transcendental nature. LSD, psilocybin, and the other hallucinogens do indeed, as Albert Hofmann asserts, constitute "cracks" in the edifice of materialistic rationality, cracks we would do well to explore and perhaps widen.

As a writer, it gives me great satisfaction to know that by this book the American reader interested in hallucinogens will be introduced to the work of Rudolf Gelpke, Ernst Jünger, and Walter Vogt, writers who are all but unknown here. With the notable exceptions of Huxley and Wasson, English and American writers on the hallucinogenic experience have been far less distinguished and eloquent than they.

This translation has been carefully overseen by Albert Hofmann, which made my task both simpler and more enjoyable.

I am beholden to R. Gordon Wasson for checking the chapters on LSD's "Mexican relatives" and on "Ska Maria Pastora" for accuracy and style.

Two chapters of this book—"How LSD Originated" and "LSD Experience and Reality"—were presented by Albert Hofmann as a paper before the international conference "Hallucinogens, Shamanism and Modern Life" in San Francisco on the afternoon of Saturday, September 30, 1978. As a part of the conference proceedings, the first chapter has been published in the *Journal of Psychedelic Drugs*, Vol. 11 (1-2), 1979.

JONATHAN OTT

Vashon Island, Washington

LSD: My Problem Child

Reflections on Sacred Drugs, Mysticism, and Science

Albert Hofmann, Ph.D.

Introduction

THERE ARE EXPERIENCES that most of us are hesitant to speak about, because they do not conform to everyday reality and defy rational explanation. These are not particular external occurrences, but rather events of our inner lives, which are generally dismissed as figments of the imagination and barred from our memory. Suddenly, the familiar view of our surroundings is transformed in a strange, delightful, or alarming way: it appears to us in a new light, takes on a special meaning. Such an experience can be as light and fleeting as a breath of air, or it can imprint itself deeply upon our minds.

One enchantment of that kind, which I experienced in childhood, has remained remarkably vivid in my memory ever since. It happened on a May morning—I have forgotten the year—but I can still point to the exact spot where it occurred, on a forest path on Martinsberg above Baden, Switzerland. As I strolled through the freshly greened woods filled with birdsong and lit up by the morning sun, all at once everything appeared in an uncommonly clear light. Was this something I had simply failed to notice before? Was I suddenly discovering the spring forest as it actually looked? It shone with the most beautiful radiance, speaking to the heart, as though it wanted to encompass me in its majesty. I was filled with an indescribable sensation of joy, oneness, and blissful security.

I have no idea how long I stood there spellbound. But I recall the anxious concern I felt as the radiance slowly dissolved and I hiked on: how could a vision that was so real and convincing, so directly and deeply felt - how could it end so soon? And how could I tell anyone about it, as my overflowing joy compelled me to do, since I knew there were no words to describe what I had seen? It seemed strange that I, as a child, had seen something so marvelous, something that adults obviously did not perceive - for I had never heard them mention it.

While still a child, I experienced several more of these deeply euphoric moments on my rambles through forest and meadow. It was these experiences that shaped the main outlines of my worldview and convinced me of the existence of a miraculous, powerful, unfathomable reality that was hidden from everyday sight.

I was often troubled in those days, wondering if I would ever, as an adult, be able to communicate these experiences; whether I would have the chance to depict my visions in poetry or paintings. But knowing that I was not cut out to be a poet or artist, I assumed I would have to keep these experiences to myself, important as they were to me.

Unexpectedly—though scarcely by chance—much later, in middle age, a link was established between my profession and these visionary experiences from childhood.

Because I wanted to gain insight into the structure and essence of matter, I became a research chemist. Intrigued by the plant world since early childhood, I chose to specialize in research on the constituents of medicinal plants. In the course of this career I was led to the psychoactive, hallucination-causing substances, which under certain conditions can evoke visionary states similar to the spontaneous experiences just described. The most important of these hallucinogenic substances has come to be known as LSD. Hallucinogens, as active compounds of considerable scientific interest, have gained entry into medicinal research, biology, and psychiatry, and later—especially LSD—also obtained wide diffusion in the drug culture.

In studying the literature connected with my work, I became

aware of the great universal significance of visionary experience. It plays a dominant role, not only in mysticism and the history of religion, but also in the creative process in art, literature, and science. More recent investigations have shown that many persons also have visionary experiences in daily life, though most of us fail to recognize their meaning and value. Mystical experiences, like those that marked my childhood, are apparently far from rare.

There is today a widespread striving for mystical experience, for visionary breakthroughs to a deeper, more comprehensive reality than that perceived by our rational, everyday consciousness. Efforts to transcend our materialistic worldview are being made in various ways, not only by the adherents of Eastern religious movements, but also by professional psychiatrists, who are adopting such profound spiritual experiences as a basic therapeutic principle.

I share the belief of many of my contemporaries that the spiritual crisis pervading all spheres of Western industrial society can be remedied only by a change in our worldview. We shall have to shift from the materialistic, dualistic belief that people and their environment are separate, toward a new consciousness of an all-encompassing reality, which embraces the experiencing ego, a reality in which people feel their oneness with animate nature and all of creation.

Everything that can contribute to such a fundamental alteration in our perception of reality must therefore command earnest attention. Foremost among such approaches are the various methods of meditation, either in a religious or a secular context, which aim to deepen the consciousness of reality by way of a total mystical experience. Another important, but still controversial, path to the same goal is the use of the consciousness-altering properties of hallucinogenic psychopharmaceuticals. LSD finds such an application in medicine, by helping patients in psychoanalysis and psychotherapy to perceive their problems in their true significance.

Deliberate provocation of mystical experience, particularly by LSD and related hallucinogens, in contrast to spontaneous visionary experiences, entails dangers that must not be underestimated. Practitioners must take into account the peculiar effects of these substances, namely their ability to influence our consciousness, the innermost essence of our being. The history of LSD to date amply demonstrates the catastrophic consequences that can ensue when its profound effect is misjudged and the substance is mistaken for a pleasure drug. Special internal and external advance preparations are required; with them, an LSD experiment can become a meaningful experience. Wrong and inappropriate use has caused LSD to become my problem child.

It is my desire in this book to give a comprehensive picture of LSD, its origin, its effects, and its dangers, in order to guard against increasing abuse of this extraordinary drug. I hope thereby to emphasize possible uses of LSD that are compatible with its characteristic action. I believe that if people would learn to use LSD's vision-inducing capability more wisely, under suitable conditions, in medical practice and in conjunction with meditation, then in the future this problem child could become a wonder child.

Chapter 1
How LSD Originated

In the realm of scientific observation,
luck is granted only to
those who are prepared.
– Louis Pasteur

TIME AND AGAIN I hear or read that LSD was discovered by
accident. This is only partly true. LSD came into being within
a systematic research program, and the "accident" did not occur
until much later. when LSD was already five years old, I happened
to experience its unforeseeable effects in my own body—or rather,
in my own mind.

Looking back over my professional career to trace the
influential events and decisions that eventually steered my work
toward the synthesis of LSD, I realize that the most decisive step
was my choice of employment upon completion of my chemistry
studies. If that decision had been different, then this substance,
which has become known the world over, might never have been
created. In order to tell the story of the origin of LSD, then, I
must also touch briefly on my career as a chemist, since the two
developments are inextricably interreleted.

In the spring of 1929, on concluding my chemistry studies
at the University of Zurich, I joined the Sandoz Company's
pharmaceutical-chemical research laboratory in Basel, as a
co-worker with Professor Arthur Stoll, founder and director of

the pharmaceutical department. I chose this position because
it afforded me the opportunity to work on natural products,
whereas two other job offers from chemical firms in Basel had
involved work in the field of synthetic chemistry.

FIRST CHEMICAL EXPLORATIONS

My doctoral work at Zurich under Professor Paul Karrer had
already given me one chance to pursue my interest in plant and
animal chemistry. Making use of the gastrointestinal juice of
the vineyard snail, I accomplished the enzymatic degradation
of chitin, the structural material of which the shells, wings,
and claws of insects, crustaceans, and other lower animals are
composed. I was able to derive the chemical structure of chitin
from the cleavage product, a nitrogen-containing sugar, obtained
by this degradation. Chitin turned out to be an analogue of
cellulose, the structural material of plants. This important result,
obtained after only three months of research, led to a doctoral
thesis rated "with distiction."

When I joined the Sandoz firm, the staff of the pharmaceutical-
chemical department was still rather modest in number. Four
chemists with doctoral degrees worked in research, three in
production.

In Stoll's laboratory I found employment that completely
agreed with me as a research chemist. The objective that
Professor Stoll had set for his pharmaceutical-chemical research
laboratories was to isolate the active principles (i.e., The effective
constituents) of known medicinal plants to produce pure
specimens of these substances. This is particularly important in
the case of medicinal plants whose active principles are unstable,
or whose potency is subject to great variation, which makes
an exact dosage difficult. But if the active principle is available
in pure form, it becomes possible to manufacture a stable
pharmaceutical preparation, exactly quantifiable by weight. With
this in mind, Professor Stoll had elected to study plant substances

of recognized value such as the substances from foxglove
(*Digitalis*), Mediterranean squill (*Scilla maritima*), and ergot of rye
(*Claviceps purpurea or Secale cornutum*), which, owning to their
instability and uncertain dosage, had been little used in medicine.

My first years in the Sandoz laboratories were devoted almost
exclusively to studying the active principles of Mediterranean
squill. Dr. Walter Kreis, one of Professor Stoll's earliest associates,
launched me in this field of research. The most important
constituents of Mediterranean squill already existed in pure form.
Their active agents, as well as those of woolly foxglove (*Digitalis
lanata*), had been isolated and purified, chiefly by Dr. Kreis, with
extraordinary skill.

The active principles of Mediterranean squill belong to the
group of cardioactive glycosides (a glycoside is a sugar-containing
substance) and serve, as do those of foxglove, in the treatment
of cardiac insufficiency. The cardiac glycosides are extremely
active substances. Because the therapeutic and the toxic doses
differ so little, it becomes especially important here to have an
exact dosage, based on pure compounds. At the beginning of my
investigations, a pharmaceutical preparation with *Scilla* glycosides
had already been introduced into therapeutics by Sandoz;
however, the chemical structure of these active compounds, with
the exception of the sugar portion, remained largely unknown.

My main contribution to the *Scilla* research, in which I
participated with enthusiasm, was to elucidate the chemical
structure of the common nucleus of *Scilla* glycosides, showing on
the one hand their differences from the *Digitalis* glycosides, and
on the other hand their close structural relationship with the
toxic principles isolated from skin glands of toads. In 1935, these
studies were temporarily concluded.

Looking for a new field of research, I asked Professor Stoll to
let me continue the investigations on the alkaloids of ergot, which
he had begun in 1917 and which had led directly to the isolation
of ergotamine in 1918. Ergotamine, discovered by Stoll, was the

first ergot alkaloid obtained in pure chemical form. Although ergotamine quickly took a significant place in therapeutics (under the trade name Gynergen) as a hemostatic remedy in obstetrics and as a medicament in the treatment of migraine, chemical research on ergot in the Sandoz laboratories was abandoned after the isolation of ergotamine and the determination of its empirical formula. Meanwhile, at the beginning of the thirties, English and American laboratories had begun to determine the chemical structure of ergot alkaloids. They had also discovered a new, water-soluble ergot alkaloid, which could likewise be isolated from the mother liquor of ergotamine production. So I thought it was high time that Sandoz resumed chemical research on ergot alkaloids, unless we wanted to risk losing our leading role in a field of medicinal research that was already becoming so important.

Professor Stoll granted my request, with some misgivings: "I must warn you of the difficulties you face in working with ergot alkaloids. These are exceedingly sensitive, easily decomposed substances, less stable than any of the compounds you have investigated in the cardiac glycoside field. But you are welcome to try." And so the switches were thrown, and I found myself engaged in a field of study that would become the main theme of my professional career. I have never forgotten the creative joy, the eager anticipation I felt in embarking on the study of ergot alkaloids, at that time a relatively uncharted field of research.

ERGOT

It may be helpful here to give some background information about ergot itself. [For further information on ergot, readers should refer to the monographs of G. Barger, *Ergot and Ergotism* (Gurney and Jackson, London, 1931) and A. Hofmann, *Die Mutterkornalkaloide* (F. Enke Verlag, Stuttgart, 1964). The former is a classical presentation of the history of the drug, while the latter emphasizes the chemical aspects.] It is produced by a lower fungus (*Claviceps purpurea*) that grows parasitically on rye, and to a lesser extent, on other species of grain and on wild grasses. Kernels infested with this fungus develop into light-brown to violet-brown curved pegs (*sclerotia*) that push forth from the husk in place of normal grains. Ergot is described botanically as a sclerotium, the form that the ergot fungus takes in winter. Ergot of rye (*Secale cornutum*) is the variety used medicinally.

Ergot, more than any other drug, has a fascinating history, in the course of which its role and meaning have been reversed: once dreaded as a poison, in the course of time it has become a rich storehouse of valuable remedies. Ergot first appeared on the stage of history in the early Middle Ages, as the cause of outbreaks of mass poisonings affecting thousands of people at a time. The illness, whose connection with ergot was for a long time obscure, appeared in two characteristic forms, one gangrenous (*ergotismus gangraenosus*) and the other convulsive (*ergotismus convulsivus*). Popular names for ergotism—such as "mal des ardents," "ignis sacer," "heiliges Feuer," or "St. Anthony's fire"—refer to the gangrenous form of the disease. The patron saint of ergotism victims was St. Anthony, and it was primarily the Order of St. Anthony that treated these patients.

Until recent times, epidemic-like outbreaks of ergot poisoning have been recorded in most European countries, including certain areas of Russia. With progress in agriculture, and since the realization, in the seventeenth century, that ergot-containing bread was the cause, the frequency and extent of ergotism epidemics diminished considerably. The last great epidemic occurred in certain areas of southern Russia in the years 1926-27. [The mass poisoning in the southern French city of Pont-St. Esprit in the year 1951, which many writers have attributed to ergot-containing bread, actually had nothing to do with ergotism. It rather involved poisoning by an organic mercury compound that was utilized for disinfecting seed.]

The first mention of a medicinal use of ergot, namely as an

ecbolic (a medicament to precipitate childbirth), is found in the herbal of the Frankfurt city physician Adam Lonitzer (Lonicerus) in the year 1582. Although ergot, as Lonitzer stated, had been used since olden times by midwives, it was not until 1808 that this drug gained entry into academic medicine, on the strength of a work by the American physician John Stearns entitled *Account of the Putvis Parturiens, a Remedy for Quickening Childbirth*. The use of ergot as an ecbolic did not, however, endure. Practitioners became aware quite early of the great danger to the child, owing primarily to the uncertainty of dosage, which when too high led to uterine spasms. From then on, the use of ergot in obstetrics was confined to stopping postpartum hemorrhage (bleeding after childbirth).

It was not until ergot's recognition in various pharmacopoeias during the first half of the nineteenth century that the first steps were taken toward isolating the active principles of the drug. However, of all the researchers who assayed this problem during the first hundred years, not one succeeded in identifying the actual substances responsible for the therapeutic activity. In 1907, the Englishmen G. Barger and F. H. Carr were the first to isolate an active alkaloidal preparation, which they named ergotoxine because it produced more of the toxic than therapeutic properties of ergot. (This preparation was not homogeneous, but rather a mixture of several alkaloids, as I was able to show thirty-five years later.) Nevertheless, the pharmacologist H. H. Dale discovered that ergotoxine, besides the uterotonic effect, also had an antagonistic activity on adrenaline in the autonomic nervous system that could lead to the therapeutic use of ergot alkaloids. Only with the isolation of ergotamine by A. Stoll (as mentioned previously) did an ergot alkaloid find entry and widespread use in therapeutics.

The early 1930s brought a new era in ergot research, beginning with the determination of the chemical structure of ergot alkaloids, as mentioned, in English and American laboratories. By chemical cleavage, W. A. Jacobs and L. C. Craig of the Rockefeller

Institute of New York succeeded in isolating and characterizing the nucleus common to all ergot alkaloids. They named it lysergic acid. Then came a major development, both for chemistry and for medicine: the isolation of the specifically uterotonic, hemostatic principle of ergot, which was published simultaneously and quite independently by four institutions, including the Sandoz laboratories. The substance, an alkaloid of comparatively simple structure, was named ergobasine (syn. ergometrine, ergonovine) by A. Stoll and E. Burckhardt. By the chemical degradation of ergobasine, W. A. Jacobs and L. C. Craig obtained lysergic acid and the amino alcohol propanolamine as cleavage products.

I set as my first goal the problem of preparing this alkaloid synthetically, through chemical linking of the two components of ergobasine, lysergic acid and propanolamine (see structural formulas in the appendix).

The lysergic acid necessary for these studies had to be obtained by chemical cleavage of some other ergot alkaloid. Since only ergotamine was available as a pure alkaloid, and was already being produced in kilogram quantities in the pharmaceutical production department, I chose this alkaloid as the starting material for my work. I set about obtaining 0.5 g of ergotamine from the ergot production people. When I sent the internal requisition form to Professor Stoll for his countersignature, he appeared in my laboratory and reproved me: "If you want to work with ergot alkaloids, you will have to familiarize yourself with the techniques of microchemistry. I can't have you consuming such a large amount of my expensive ergotamine for your experiments."

The ergot production department, besides using ergot of Swiss origin to obtain ergotamine, also dealt with Portuguese ergot, which yielded an amorphous alkaloidal preparation that corresponded to the aforementioned ergotoxine first produced by Barger and Carr. I decided to use this less expensive material for the preparation of lysergic acid. The alkaloid obtained from the production department had to be purified further before it would be suitable for cleavage to lysergic acid. Observations made during the purification process led me to think that ergotoxine could be a mixture of several alkaloids, rather than one homogeneous alkaloid. I will speak later of the far-reaching sequelae of these observations.

Here I must digress briefly to describe the working conditions and techniques that prevailed in those days. These remarks may be of interest to the present generation of research chemists in industry, who are accustomed to far better conditions.

We were very frugal. Individual laboratories were considered a rare extravagance. During the first six years of my employment with Sandoz, I shared a laboratory with two colleagues. We three chemists, plus an assistant each, worked in the same room on three different fields: Dr. Kreiss on cardiac glycosides; Dr. Wiedemann, who joined Sandoz around the same time as I, on the leaf pigment chlorophyll; and I ultimately on ergot alkaloids. The laboratory was equipped with two fume hoods (compartments supplied with outlets), providing less than effective ventilation by gas flames. When we requested that these hoods be equipped with ventilators, our chief refused on the ground that ventilation by gas flame had sufficed in Willstatter's laboratory.

During the last years of World War I, Professor Stoll had been an assistant in Berlin and Munich to the world-famous chemist and Nobel laureate Professor Richard Willstatter, and with him had conducted the fundamental investigations on chlorophyll and the assimilation of carbon dioxide. There was scarcely a scientific discussion with Professor Stoll in which he did not mention his revered teacher Professor Willstatter and his work in Willstatter's laboratory.

The working techniques available to chemists in the field of organic chemistry at that time (the beginning of the thirties) were essentially the same as those employed by Justus von Liebig a hundred years earlier. The most important development achieved since then was the introduction of microanalysis by

B. Pregl, which made it possible to ascertain the elemental composition of a compound with only a few milligrams of specimen, whereas earlier a few centigrams were needed. Of the other physical-chemical techniques at the disposal of the chemist today—techniques which have changed his way of working, making it faster and more effective, and created entirely new possibilities, above all for the elucidation of structure—none yet existed in those days.

For the investigations of *Scilla* glycosides and the first studies in the ergot field, I still used the old separation and purification techniques from Liebig's day: fractional extraction, fractional precipitation, fractional crystallization, and the like. The introduction of column chromatography, the first important step in modern laboratory technique, was of great value to me only in later investigations. For structure determination, which today can be conducted rapidly and elegantly with the help of spectroscopic methods (UV, IR, NMR) and X-ray crystallography, we had to rely, in the first fundamental ergot studies, entirely on the old laborious methods of chemical degradation and derivatization.

LYSERGIC ACID AND ITS DERIVATIVES

Lysergic acid proved to be a rather unstable substance, and its rebonding with basic radicals posed difficulties. In the technique known as Curtius' Synthesis, I ultimately found a process that proved useful for combining lysergic acid with amines. With this method I produced a great number of lysergic acid compounds. By combining lysergic acid with the amino alcohol propanolamine, I obtained a compound that was identical to the natural ergot alkaloid ergobasine. With that, the first synthesis—that is, artificial production—of an ergot alkaloid was accomplished. This was not only of scientific interest, as confirmation of the chemical structure of ergobasine, which was valuable in obstetrics.

After this first success in the ergot field, my investigations went forward on two fronts. First, I attempted to improve the pharmacological properties of ergobasine by variations of its amino alcohol radical. My colleague Dr. J. Peyer and I developed a process for the economical production of propanolamine and other amino alcohols. Indeed, by substitution of the propanolamine contained in ergobasine with the amino alcohol butanolamine, an active principle was obtained that even surpassed the natural alkaloid in its therapeutic properties. This improved ergobasine has found worldwide application as a dependable uterotonic, hemostatic remedy under the trade name Methergine, and is today the leading medicament for this indication in obstetrics.

I further employed my synthetic procedure to produce new lysergic acid compounds for which uterotonic activity was not prominent, but from which, on the basis of their chemical structure, other types of interesting pharmacological properties could be expected. In 1938, I produced the twenty-fifth substance in this series of lysergic acid derivatives: lysergic acid diethylamide, abbreviated LSD-25 (*Lyserg-saure-diathylamid*) for laboratory usage. I had planned the synthesis of this compound with the intention of obtaining a circulatory and respiratory stimulant (an analeptic). Such stimulating properties could be expected for lysergic acid diethylamide, because it shows similarity in chemical structure to the analeptic already known at that time, namely nicotinic acid diethylamide (Coramine). During the testing of LSD-25 in the pharmacological department of Sandoz, whose director at the time was Professor Ernst Rothlin, a strong effect on the uterus was established. It amounted to some 70 percent of the activity of ergobasine. The research report also noted, in passing, that the experimental animals became restless during the narcosis. The new substance, however, aroused no special interest in our pharmacologists and physicians; testing was therefore discontinued.

For the next five years, nothing more was heard of the substance LSD-25. Meanwhile, my work in the ergot field advanced further in other areas. Through the purification of ergotoxine, the starting material for lysergic acid, I obtained, as already mentioned, the impression that this alkaloidal preparation was not homogeneous, but was rather a mixture of different substances. This doubt as to the homogeneity of ergotoxine was reinforced when in its hydrogenation two distinctly different hydrogenation products were obtained, whereas the homogeneous alkaloid ergotamine under the same condition yielded only a single hydrogenation product (hydrogenation is the introduction of hydrogen).

Extended, systematic analytical investigations of the supposed ergotoxine mixture led ultimately to the separation of this alkaloidal preparation into three homogeneous components. One of the three chemically homogeneous ergotoxine alkaloids proved to be identical with an alkaloid isolated shortly before in the production department, which A. Stoll and E. Burckhardt had named ergocristine. The other two alkaloids were both new. The first I named ergocornine; and for the second, the last to be isolated, which had long remained hidden in the mother liquor, I chose the name ergokryptine (kryptos meaning hidden). Later it was found that ergokryptine occurs in two isomeric forms, which were differentiated as alpha- and beta-ergokryptine.

The solution of the ergotoxine problem was not merely scientifically interesting, but also had great practical significance. A valuable remedy arose from it. The three hydrogenated ergotoxine alkaloids that I produced in the course of these investigations, dihydroergocristine, dihydroergokryptine, and dihydroergocornine, displayed medicinally useful properties during testing by Professor Rothlin in the pharmacological department. From these three substances, the pharmaceutical preparation Hydergine was developed, a medicament for improvement of peripheral circulation and cerebral function in the control of geriatric disorders. Hydergine has proven to be an effective remedy in geriatrics for these indications. Today it is

Sandoz's most important pharmaceutical product.

Dihydroergotamine, which I likewise produced in the course of these investigations, has also found application in therapeutics as a circulation- and blood-pressure-stabilizing medicament, under the trade name Dihydergot.

While today research on important projects is almost exclusively carried out as teamwork, the investigations on ergot alkaloids described above were conducted by myself alone.

Even the further chemical steps in the evolution of commercial preparations remained in my hands—that is, the preparation of larger specimens for the clinical trials, and finally the perfection of the first procedures for mass production of Methergine, Hydergine, and Dihydergot. This even included the analytical controls for the development of the first galenical forms of these three preparations: the ampules, liquid solutions, and tablets. My aides at that time included a laboratory assistant, a laboratory helper, and later in addition a second laboratory assistant and a chemical technician.

DISCOVERY OF THE PSYCHIC EFFECTS OF LSD

The solution of the ergotoxine problem had led to fruitful results, described here only briefly, and had opened up further avenues of research. And yet I could not forget the relatively uninteresting LSD-25. A peculiar presentiment—the feeling that this substance could possess properties other than those established in the first investigations—induced me, five years after the first synthesis, to produce LSD-25 once again so that a sample could be given to the pharmacological department for further tests. This was quite unusual; experimental substances, as a rule, were definitely stricken from the research program if once found to be lacking in pharmacological interest.

Nevertheless, in the spring of 1943, I repeated the synthesis of LSD-25. As in the first synthesis, this involved the production of only a few centigrams of the compound.

In the final step of the synthesis, during the purification and crystallization of lysergic acid diethylamide in the form of a tartrate (tartaric acid salt), I was interrupted in my work by unusual sensations. The following description of this incident comes from the report that I sent at the time to Professor Stoll:

Last Friday, April 16,1943, I was forced to interrupt my work in the laboratory in the middle of the afternoon and proceed home, being affected by a remarkable restlessness, combined with a slight dizziness. At home I lay down and sank into a not unpleasant intoxicated-like condition,characterized by an extremely stimulated imagination. In a dreamlike state, with eyes closed (I found the daylight to be unpleasantly glaring), I perceived an uninterrupted stream of fantastic pictures, extraordinary shapes with intense, kaleidoscopic play of colors. After some two hours this condition faded away.

This was, altogether, a remarkable experience—both in its sudden onset and its extraordinary course. It seemed to have resulted from some external toxic influence; I surmised a connection with the substance I had been working with at the time, lysergic acid diethylamide tartrate. But this led to another question: how had I managed to absorb this material?

Because of the known toxicity of ergot substances, I always maintained meticulously neat work habits. Possibly a bit of the LSD solution had contacted my fingertips during crystallization, and a trace of the substance was absorbed through the skin. If LSD-25 had indeed been the cause of this bizarre experience, then it must be a substance of extraordinary potency. There seemed to be only one way of getting to the bottom of this. I decided on a self-experiment.

Exercising extreme caution, I began the planned series of experiments with the smallest quantity that could be expected to produce some effect, considering the activity of the ergot alkaloids known at the time: namely, 0.25 mg (mg = milligram =

one thousandth of a gram) of lysergic acid diethylamide tartrate. Quoted below is the entry for this experiment in my laboratory journal of April 19, 1943.

SELF-EXPERIMENTS

> *4/19/43 16:20: 0.5 cc of 1/2 promil aqueous solution of diethylamide tartrate orally = 0.25 mg tartrate. Taken diluted with about 10 cc water. Tasteless. 17:00: Beginning dizziness, feeling of anxiety, visual distortions, symptoms of paralysis, desire to laugh. Supplement of 4/21: Home by bicycle. From 18:00- ca.20:00 most severe crisis. (See special report.)*

Here the notes in my laboratory journal cease. I was able to write the last words only with great effort. By now it was already clear to me that LSD had been the cause of the remarkable experience of the previous Friday, for the altered perceptions were of the same type as before, only much more intense. I had to struggle to speak intelligibly. I asked my laboratory assistant, who was informed of the self-experiment, to escort me home. We went by bicycle, no automobile being available because of wartime restrictions on their use. On the way home, my condition began to assume threatening forms. Everything in my field of vision wavered and was distorted as if seen in a curved mirror. I also had the sensation of being unable to move from the spot. Nevertheless, my assistant later told me that we had traveled very rapidly. Finally, we arrived at home safe and sound, and I was just barely capable of asking my companion to summon our family doctor and request milk from the neighbors.

In spite of my delirious, bewildered condition, I had brief periods of clear and effective thinking—and chose milk as a nonspecific antidote for poisoning. The dizziness and sensation of fainting became so strong at times that I could no longer hold myself erect, and had to lie down on a sofa. My surroundings had now transformed themselves in more terrifying ways.

Everything in the room spun around, and the familiar objects and pieces of furniture assumed grotesque, threatening forrns. They were in continuous motion, animated, as if driven by an inner restlessness. The lady next door, whom I scarcely recognized, brought me milk—in the course of the evening I drank more than two liters. She was no longer Mrs. R., but rather a malevolent, insidious witch with a colored mask.

Even worse than these demonic transformations of the outer world were the alterations that I perceived in myself, in my inner being. Every exertion of my will, every attempt to put an end to the disintegration of the outer world and the dissolution of my ego, seemed to be wasted effort. A demon had invaded me, had taken possession of my body, mind, and soul. I jumped up and screamed, trying to free myself from him, but then sank down again and lay helpless on the sofa. The substance, with which I had wanted to experiment, had vanquished me. It was the demon that scornfully triumphed over my will. I was seized by the dreadful fear of going insane. I was taken to another world, another place, another time. My body seemed to be without sensation, lifeless, strange. Was I dying? Was this the transition? At times I believed myself to be outside my body, and then perceived clearly, as an outside observer, the complete tragedy of my situation. I had not even taken leave of my family (my wife, with our three children, had traveled that day to visit her parents in Lucerne). Would they ever understand that I had not experimented thoughtlessly, irresponsibly, but rather with the utmost caution, and that such a result was in no way foreseeable? My fear and despair intensified, not only because a young family should lose its father, but also because I dreaded leaving my chemical research work, which meant so much to me, unfinished in the midst of fruitful, promising development. Another reflection took shape, an idea full of bitter irony: if I was now forced to leave this world prematurely, it was because of this lysergic acid diethylamide that I myself had brought forth into the world.

By the time the doctor arrived, the climax of my despondent condition had already passed. My laboratory assistant informed him about my self-experiment, as I myself was not yet able to formulate a coherent sentence. He shook his head in perplexity, after my attempts to describe the mortal danger that threatened my body. He could detect no abnormal symptoms other than extremely dilated pupils. Pulse, blood pressure, breathing were all normal. He saw no reason to prescribe any medication. Instead he conveyed me to my bed and stood watch over me. Slowly I came back from a weird, unfamiliar world to reassuring everyday reality. The horror softened and gave way to a feeling of good fortune and gratitude, the more normal perceptions and thoughts returned, and I became more confident that the danger of insanity was conclusively past.

Now, little by little I could begin to enjoy the unprecedented colors and plays of shapes that persisted behind my closed eyes. Kaleidoscopic, fantastic images surged in on me, alternating, variegated, opening and then closing themselves in circles and spirals, exploding in colored fountains, rearranging and hybridizing themselves in constant flux. It was particularly remarkable how every acoustic perception, such as the sound of a door handle or a passing automobile, became transformed into optical perceptions. Every sound generated a vividly changing image, with its own consistent form and color.

Late in the evening my wife returned from Lucerne. Someone had informed her by telephone that I was suffering a mysterious breakdown. She had returned home at once, leaving the children behind with her parents. By now, I had recovered myself sufficiently to tell her what had happened.

Exhausted, I then slept, to awake next morning refreshed, with a clear head, though still somewhat tired physically. A sensation of well-being and renewed life flowed through me. Breakfast tasted delicious and gave me extraordinary pleasure. When I later

walked out into the garden, in which the sun shone now after
a spring rain, everything glistened and sparkled in a fresh light.
The world was as if newly created. All my senses vibrated in a
condition of highest sensitivity, which persisted for the entire day.

This self-experiment showed that LSD-25 behaved as a
psychoactive substance with extraordinary properties and
potency. There was to my knowledge no other known substance
that evoked such profound psychic effects in such extremely low
doses, that caused such dramatic changes in human consciousness
and our experience of the inner and outer world.

What seemed even more significant was that I could remember
the experience of LSD inebriation in every detail. This could only
mean that the conscious recording function was not interrupted,
even in the climax of the LSD experience, despite the profound
breakdown of the normal worldview. For the entire duration of
the experiment, I had even been aware of participating in an
experiment, but despite this recognition of my condition, I could
not, with every exertion of my will, shake off the LSD world.
Everything was experienced as completely real, as alarming
reality, alarming, because the picture of the other, familiar
everyday reality was still fully preserved in the memory for
comparison.

Another surprising aspect of LSD was its ability to produce
such a far-reaching, powerful state of inebriation without
leaving a hangover. Quite the contrary, on the day after the LSD
experiment I felt myself to be, as already described, in excellent
physical and mental condition.

I was aware that LSD, a new active compound with such
properties, would have to be of use in pharmacology, in
neurology, and especially in psychiatry, and that it would attract
the interest of concerned specialists. But at that time I had no
inkling that the new substance would also come to be used
beyond medical science, as an inebriant in the drug scene.

Since my self-experiment had revealed LSD in its terrifying, demonic aspect, the last thing I could have expected was that this substance could ever find application as anything approaching a pleasure drug. I failed, moreover, to recognize the meaningful connection between LSD inebriation and spontaneous visionary experience until much later, after further experiments, which were carried out with far lower doses and under different conditions.

The next day I wrote to Professor Stoll the abovementioned report about my extraordinary experience with LSD-25 and sent a copy to the director of the pharmacological department, Professor Rothlin.

As expected, the first reaction was incredulous astonishment. Instantly a telephone call came from the management; Professor Stoll asked: "Are you certain you made no mistake in the weighing? Is the stated dose really correct?" Professor Rothlin also called, asking the same question. I was certain of this point, for I had executed the weighing and dosage with my own hands. Yet their doubts were justified to some extent, for until then no known substance had displayed even the slightest psychic effect in fraction-of-a-milligram doses. An active compound of such potency seemed almost unbelievable.

Professor Rothlin himself and two of his colleagues were the first to repeat my experiment, with only one-third of the dose I had utilized. But even at that level, the effects were still extremely impressive, and quite fantastic. All doubts about the statements in my report were eliminated.

Chapter 2
LSD in Animal Experiments and Biological Research

AFTER THE DISCOVERY of its extraordinary psychic effects, the substance LSD-25, which five years earlier had been excluded from further investigation after the first trials on animals, was again admitted into the series of experimental preparations. Most of the fundamental studies on animals were carried out by Dr. Aurelio Cerletti in the Sandoz pharmacological department, headed by Professor Rothlin.

Before a new active substance can be investigated in systematic clinical trials with human subjects, extensive data on its effects and side effects must be determined in pharmacological tests on animals. These experiments must assay the assimilation and elimination of the particular substance in organisms, and above all its tolerance and relative toxicity. Only the most important reports on animal experiments with LSD, and those intelligible to the layperson, will be reviewed here. It would greatly exceed the scope of this book if I attempted to mention all the results of several hundred pharmacological investigations, which have been conducted all over the world in connection with the fundamental work on LSD in the Sandoz laboratories.

Animal experiments reveal little about the mental alterations caused by LSD because psychic effects are scarcely determinable in lower animals, and even in the more highly developed, they can be established only to a limited extent. LSD produces its effects above all in the sphere of the higher and highest psychic and intellectual functions. It is therefore understandable that specific reactions to LSD can be expected only in higher animals.

Subtle psychic changes cannot be established in animals because, even if they should be occurring, the animal could not give them expression. Thus, only relatively heavy psychic disturbances, expressing themselves in the altered behavior of research animals, become discernible. Quantities that are substantially higher than the effective dose of LSD in human beings are therefore necessary, even in higher animals like cats, dogs, and apes.

While the mouse under LSD shows only motor disturbances and alterations in licking behavior, in the cat we see, besides vegetative symptoms like bristling of the hair (piloerection) and salivation, indications that point to the existence of hallucinations. The animals stare anxiously in the air, and instead of attacking the mouse, the cat leaves it alone or will even stand in fear before the mouse. One could also conclude that the behavior of dogs that are under the influence of LSD involves hallucinations. A caged community of chimpanzees reacts very sensitively if a member of the tribe has received LSD. Even though no changes appear in this single animal, the whole cage gets in an uproar because the LSD chimpanzee no longer observes the laws of its finely coordinated hierarchic tribal order.

Of the remaining animal species on which LSD was tested, only aquarium fish and spiders need be mentioned here. In the fish, unusual swimming postures were observed, and in the spiders, alterations in web building were apparently produced by LSD. At very low optimum doses the webs were even better proportioned and more exactly built than normally; however, with higher doses, the webs were badly and rudimentarily made.

How Toxic Is LSD?

The toxicity of LSD has been determined in various animal species. A standard for the toxicity of a substance is the LD50, or the median lethal dose, that is, the dose with which 50 percent of the treated animals die. In general it fluctuates broadly, according to the animal species, and so it is with LSD. The LD50 for the mouse amounts to 50-60 mg/kg IV (that is, 50 to 60 thousandths of a gram of LSD per kilogram of animal weight upon injection of an LSD solution into the veins). In the rat the LD50 drops to 16.5 mg/kg, and in rabbits to 0.3 mg/kg. One elephant given 0.297 g of LSD died after a few minutes. The weight of this animal was determined to be 5,000 kg, which corresponds to a lethal dose of 0.06 mg/kg (0.06 thousandths of a gram per kilogram of body weight). Because this involves only a single case, this value cannot be generalized, but we can at least deduce from it that the largest land animal reacts proportionally very sensitively to LSD, since the lethal dose in elephants must be some 1,000 times lower than in the mouse. Most animals die from a lethal dose of LSD by respiratory arrest.

The minute doses that cause death in animal experiments may give the impression that LSD is a very toxic substance. However, if one compares the lethal dose in animals with the effective dose in human beings, which is 0.0003-0.001 mg/kg (0.0003 to 0.001 thousandths of a gram per kilogram of body weight), this shows an extraordinarily low toxicity for LSD. Only a 300- to 600-fold overdose of LSD, compared to the lethal dose in rabbits, or fully a 50,000- to 100,000-fold overdose, in comparison to the toxicity in the mouse, would have fatal results in human beings. These comparisons of relative toxicity are, to be sure, only understandable as estimates of orders of magnitude, for the determination of the therapeutic index (that is, the ratio between the effective and the lethal dose) is only meaningful within a given species. Such a procedure is not possible in this case because the lethal dose of LSD for humans is not known. To my knowledge, there have not as yet occurred any casualties that are a direct consequence of LSD poisoning. Numerous episodes of fatal consequences attributed to LSD ingestion have indeed been recorded, but these were accidents, even suicides, that may be attributed to the mentally disoriented condition of LSD intoxication. The danger of LSD lies not in its toxicity, but rather in the unpredictability of its psychic effects.

Some years ago reports appeared in the scientific literature and also in the lay press, alleging that damage to chromosomes or the genetic material had been caused by LSD. These effects, however, have been observed in only a few individual cases. Subsequent comprehensive investigations of a large, statistically significant number of cases, however, showed that there was no connection between chromosome anomalies and LSD medication. The same applies to reports about fetal deformities that had allegedly been produced by LSD. In animal experiments, it is indeed possible to induce fetal deformities through extremely high doses of LSD, which lie well above the doses used in human beings. But under these conditions, even harmless substances produce such damage. Examination of reported individual cases of human fetal deformities reveals, again, no connection between LSD use and such injury. If there had been any such connection, it would long since have attracted attention, for several million people by now have taken LSD.

PHARMACOLOGICAL PROPERTIES OF LSD

LSD is absorbed easily and completely through the gastrointestinal tract. It is therefore unnecessary to inject LSD, except for special purposes. Experiments on mice with radioactively labeled LSD have established that intravenously injected LSD disappeared, down to a small vestige, very rapidly from the bloodstream and was distributed throughout the organism. Unexpectedly, the lowest concentration is found in the brain. It is concentrated here in certain centers of the midbrain that play a role in the regulation of emotion. Such findings give indications as to the localization of certain psychic functions in the brain.

The concentration of LSD in the various organs attains maximum values 10 to 15 minutes after injection, then falls off again swiftly. The small intestine, in which the concentration attains the maximum within two hours, constitutes an exception. The elimination of LSD is conducted for the most part (up to some 80 percent) through the intestine via liver and bile. Only one to 10 percent of the elimination product exists as unaltered LSD; the remainder is made up of various transformation products.

As the psychic effects of LSD persist even after it can no longer be detected in the organism, we must assume that LSD is not active as such, but that it rather triggers certain biochemical, neurophysiological, and psychic mechanisms that provoke the inebriated condition and continue in the absence of the active principle.

LSD stimulates centers of the sympathetic nervous system in the midbrain, which leads to pupillary dilatation, increase in body temperature, and rise in the blood-sugar level. The uterine-constricting activity of LSD has already been mentioned.

An especially interesting pharmacological property of LSD, discovered by J. H. Gaddum in England, is its serotonin-blocking effect. Serotonin is a hormone-like substance, occurring naturally in various organs of warm-blooded animals. Concentrated in the midbrain, it plays an important role in the propagation of impulses in certain nerves and therefore in the biochemistry of psychic functions. The disruption of natural functioning of serotonin by LSD was for some time regarded as an explanation of its psychic effects. However, it was soon shown that even certain derivatives of LSD (compounds in which the chemical structure of LSD is slightly modified), that exhibit no hallucinogenic properties, inhibit the effects of serotonin just as strongly, or yet more strongly, than unaltered LSD. The serotonin-blocking effect of LSD thus does not suffice to explain its hallucinogenic properties.

LSD also influences neurophysiological functions that are connected with dopamine, which is, like serotonin, a naturally occurring hormone-like substance. Most of the brain centers receptive to dopamine become activated by LSD, while the others are depressed.

As yet we do not know the biochemical mechanisms through which LSD exerts its psychic effects. Investigations of the interactions of LSD with brain factors like serotonin and dopamine, however, are examples of how LSD can serve as a tool in brain research, in the study of the biochemical processes that underlie the psychic functions.

Chapter 3
Chemical Modifications of LSD

WHEN A NEW TYPE of active compound is discovered in
pharmaceutical-chemical research, whether by isolation from
a plant drug or from animal organs, or through synthetic
production as in the case of LSD, then the chemist attempts,
through alterations in its molecular structure, to produce
new compounds with similar, perhaps improved activity, or
with other valuable active properties. We call this process a
chemical modification of this type of active substance. Of the
approximately 20,000 new substances that are produced annually
in the pharmaceutical-chemical research laboratories of the
world, the overwhelming majority are modification products of
proportionally few types of active compounds. The discovery of a
really new type of active substance - new with regard to chemical
structure and pharmacological effect - is a rare stroke of luck.

Soon after the discovery of the psychic effects of LSD,
two coworkers were assigned to join me in carrying out the
chemical modification of LSD on a broader basis and in further
investigations in the field of ergot alkaloids. The work on the
chemical structure of ergot alkaloids of the peptide type, to which
ergotamine and the alkaloids of the ergotoxine group belong,
continued with Dr. Theodor Petrzilka. Working with Dr. Franz
Troxler, I produced a great number of chemical modifications of
LSD, and we attempted to gain further insights into the structure
of lysergic acid, for which the American researchers had already
proposed a structural formula. In 1949 we succeeded in correcting
this formula and specifying the valid structure of this common

nucleus of all ergot alkaloids, including of course LSD.

The investigations of the peptide alkaloids of ergot led to the complete structural formulas of these substances, which we published in 1951. Their correctness was confirmed through the total synthesis of ergotamine, which was realized ten years later in collaboration with two younger coworkers, Dr. Albert J. Frey and Dr. Hans Ott. Another coworker, Dr. Paul A. Stadler, was largely responsible for the development of this synthesis into a process practicable on an industrial scale. The synthetic production of peptide ergot alkaloids using lysergic acid obtained from special cultures of the ergot fungus in tanks has great economic importance. This procedure is used to produce the starting material for the medicaments Hydergine and Dihydergot.

Now we return to the chemical modifications of LSD. Many LSD derivatives were produced, since 1945, in collaboration with Dr. Troxler, but none proved hallucinogenically more active than LSD. Indeed, the very closest relatives proved themselves essentially less active in this respect.

There are four different possibilities of spatial arrangement of atoms in the LSD molecule. They are differentiated in technical language by the prefix iso- and the letters D and L. Besides LSD, which is more precisely designated as D-lysergic acid diethylamide, I have also produced and likewise tested in self-experiments the three other spatially different forms, namely D-isolysergic acid diethylamide (iso-LSD), L-lysergic acid diethylamide (L-LSD), and L-isolysergic acid diethylamide (L-iso-LSD). The last three forms of LSD showed no psychic effects up to a dose of 0.5 mg, which corresponds to a 20-fold quantity of a still distinctly active LSD dose.

A substance very closely related to LSD, the monoethylamide of lysergic acid (LAE-23), in which an ethyl group is replaced by a hydrogen atom on the diethylamide residue of LSD, proved to be some ten times less psychoactive than LSD. The hallucinogenic effect of this substance is also qualitatively different: it is characterized by a narcotic component. This narcotic effect is yet more pronounced in lysergic acid amide (LA-111), in which both ethyl groups of LSD are displaced by hydrogen atoms. These effects, which I established in comparative self-experiments with LA-111 and LAE-32, were corroborated by subsequent clinical investigations.

Fifteen years later we encountered lysergic acid amide, which had been produced synthetically for these investigations, as a naturally occurring active principle of the Mexican magic drug *ololiuhqui*. In a later chapter I shall deal more fully with this unexpected discovery.

Certain results of the chemical modification of LSD proved valuable to medicinal research; LSD derivatives were found that were only weakly or not at all hallucinogenic, but instead exhibited other effects of LSD to an increased extent. Such an effect of LSD is its blocking effect on the neurotransmitter serotonin (referred to previously in the discussion of the pharmacological properties of LSD). As serotonin plays a role in allergic-inflammatory processes and also in the generation of migraine, a specific serotonin-blocking substance was of great significance to medicinal research. We therefore searched systematically for LSD derivatives without hallucinogenic effects, but with the highest possible activity as serotonin blockers. The first such active substance was found in bromo-LSD, which has become known in medicinal-biological research under the designation BOL-148. In the course of our investigations on serotonin antagonists, Dr. Troxler produced in the sequel yet stronger and more specifically active compounds. The most active entered the medicinal market as a medicament for the treatment of migraine, under the trademark "Deseril" or, in English-speaking countries, "Sansert."

Chapter 4
Use of LSD in Psychiatry

SOON AFTER LSD was tried on animals, the first systematic investigation of the substance was carried out on human beings, at the psychiatric clinic of the University of Zurich. Werner A. Stoll, M.D. (a son of Professor Arthur Stoll), who led this research, published his results in 1947 in the *Schweizer Archiv fur Neurologie und Psychiatrie*, under the title "Lysergsaure-diathylamid, ein Phantastikum aus der Mutterkorngruppe" [Lysergic acid diethylamide, a phantasticum from the ergot group].

The tests involved healthy research subjects as well as schizophrenic patients. The dosages—substantially lower than in my first self-experiment with 0.25 mg LSD tartrate—amounted to only 0.02 to 0.13 mg. The emotional state during the LSD inebriation was here predominantly euphoric, whereas in my experiment the mood was marked by grave side effects resulting from overdosage and, of course, fear of the uncertain outcome.

This fundamental publication, which gave a scientific description of all the basic features of LSD inebriation, classified the new active principle as a phantasticum. However, the question of therapeutic application of LSD remained unanswered. On the other hand, the report emphasized the extraordinarily high activity of LSD, which corresponds to the activity of trace substances occurring in the organism that are considered to be responsible for certain mental disorders. Another subject discussed in this first publication was the possible application of LSD as a research tool in psychiatry, which follows from its tremendous psychic activity.

First Self-Experiment by a Psychiatrist

In his paper, W. A. Stoll also gave a detailed description of his own personal experiment with LSD. Since this was the first self-experiment published by a psychiatrist, and since it describes many characteristic features of LSD inebriation, it is interesting to quote extensively from the report. I warmly thank the author for kind permission to republish this extract.

> At eight o'clock I took 60 mcg (0.06 milligrams) of LSD. Some 20 minutes later, the first symptoms appeared: heaviness in the limbs, slight atactic (i.e., confused, uncoordinated) symptoms. A subjectively very unpleasant phase of general malaise followed, in parallel with the drop in blood pressure registered by the examiners.
>
> A certain euphoria then set in, though it seemed weaker to me than experiences in an earlier experiment. The ataxia increased, and I went "sailing" around the room with large strides. I felt somewhat better, but was glad to lie down.
>
> Afterward the room was darkened (dark experiment); there followed an unprecedented experience of unimaginable intensity that kept increasing in strength. It was characterized by an unbelievable profusion of optical hallucinations that appeared and vanished with great speed, to make way for countless new images. I saw a profusion of circles, vortices, sparks, showers, crosses, and spirals in constant, racing flux.
>
> The images appeared to stream in on me predominantly from the center of the visual field, or out of the lower left edge. When a picture appeared in the middle, the remaining field of vision was simultaneously filled up with a vast number of similar visions. All were colored: bright, luminous red, yellow, and green predominated.
>
> I never managed to linger on any picture. When the supervisor of the experiment emphasized my great fantasies, the richness of my statements, I could only react with a

sympathetic smile. I knew, in fact, that I could not retain,
much less describe, more than a fraction of the pictures.
I had to force myself to give a description. Terms such as
"fireworks" or "kaleidoscopic" were poor and inadequate. I
felt that I had to immerse myself more and more deeply into
this strange and fascinating world, in order to allow the
exuberance, the unimaginable wealth, to work on me.

At first, the hallucinations were elementary: rays,
bundles of rays, rain, rings, vortices, loops, sprays, clouds,
etc. Then more highly organized visions also appeared:
arches, rows of arches, a sea of roofs, desert landscapes,
terraces, flickering fire, starry skies of unbelievable splendor.
The original, more simple images continued in the midst of
these more highly organized hallucinations. I remember the
following images in particular:

A succession of towering, Gothic vaults, an endless choir,
of which I could not see the lower portions.

A landscape of skyscrapers, reminiscent of pictures of the
entrance to New York harbor: house towers staggered behind
and beside one another with innumerable rows of windows.
Again the foundation was missing.

A system of masts and ropes, which reminded me of a
reproduction of a painting seen the previous day (the inside
of a circus tent).

An evening sky of an unimaginable pale blue over
the dark roofs of a Spanish city. I had a peculiar feeling
of anticipation, was full of joy and decidedly ready for
adventure. All at once the stars flared up, amassed, and
turned to a dense rain of stars and sparks that streamed
toward me. City and sky had disappeared.

I was in a garden, saw brilliant red, yellow, and green
lights falling through a dark trelliswork, an indescribably
joyous experience.

It was significant that all the images consisted of

countless repetitions of the same elements: many sparks, many circles, many arches, many windows, many fires, etc. I never saw isolated images, but always duplications of the same image, endlessly repeated.

I felt myself one with all romanticists and dreamers, thought of E. T. A. Hoffmann, saw the maelstrom of Poe (even though, at the time I had read Poe, his description seemed exaggerated). Often I seemed to stand at the pinnacle of artistic experience; I luxuriated in the colors of the altar of Isenheim, and knew the euphoria and exultation of an artistic vision. I must also have spoken again and again of modern art; I thought of abstract pictures, which all at once I seemed to understand. Then again, there were impressions of an extreme trashiness, both in their shapes and their color combinations. The most garish, cheap modern lamp ornaments and sofa pillows came into my mind. The train of thought was quickened. But I had the feeling the supervisor of the experiment could still keep up with me. Of course I knew, intellectually, that I was rushing him. At first I had descriptions rapidly at hand. With the increasingly frenzied pace, it became impossible to think a thought through to the end. I must have only started many sentences.

When I tried to restrict myself to specific subjects, the experiment proved most unsuccessful. My mind would even focus, in a certain sense, on contrary images: skyscrapers instead of a church, a broad desert instead of a mountain.

I assumed that I had accurately estimated the elapsed time, but did not take the matter very seriously. Such questions did not interest me in the slightest.

My state of mind was consciously euphoric. I enjoyed the condition, was serene, and took a most active interest in the experience. From time to time I opened my eyes. The weak red light seemed mysterious, much more than before. The busily writing research supervisor appeared to me to

be very far away. Often I had peculiar bodily sensations: I
believed my hands to be attached to some distant body, but
was not certain whether it was my own.

After termination of the first dark experiment, I
strolled about in the room a bit, was unsure on my legs,
and again felt less well. I became cold and was thankful
that the research supervisor covered me with a blanket. I
felt unkempt, unshaven, and unwashed. The room seemed
strange and broad. Later I squatted on a high stool, thinking
all the while that I sat there like a bird on the roost.

The supervisor emphasized my own wretched
appearance. He seemed remarkably graceful. I myself had
small, finely formed hands. As I washed them, it was
happening a long way from me, somewhere down below
on the right. It was questionable, but utterly unimportant,
whether they were my own hands.

In the landscape outside, well known to me, many
things appeared to have changed. Besides the hallucinations,
I could now see the real as well. Later this was no longer
possible, although I remained aware that reality was
otherwise.

A barracks, and the garage standing before it to the
left, suddenly changed to a landscape of ruins, shattered to
pieces. I saw wall wreckage and projecting beams, inspired
undoubtedly by the memory of the war events in this region.

In a uniform, extensive field, I kept seeing figures,
which I tried to draw, but could get no farther than the
crudest beginnings. I saw an extremely opulent sculptural
ornamentation in constant metamorphosis, in continuous
flux. I was reminded of every possible foreign culture,
saw Mexican, Indian motifs. Between a grating of small
beams and tendrils appeared little caricatures, idols, masks,
strangely mixed all of a sudden with childish drawings
of people. The tempo was slackened compared to the dark

experiment.

The euphoria had now vanished. I became depressed, especially during the second dark experiment, which followed. Whereas during the first dark experiment, the hallucinations had alternated with great rapidity in bright and luminous colors, now blue, violet, and dark green prevailed. The movement of larger images was slower, milder, quieter, although even these were composed of finely raining "elemental dots," which streamed and whirled about quickly. During the first dark experiment, the commotion had frequently intruded upon me; now it often led distinctly away from me into the center of the picture, where a sucking mouth appeared. I saw grottoes with fantastic erosions and stalactites, reminding me of the child's book IM WUNDERREICHE DES BERGKONIGS [In the wondrous realm of the mountain king]. Serene systems of arches rose up. On the right-hand side, a row of shed roofs suddenly appeared; I thought of an evening ride homeward during military service. Significantly it involved a homeward ride: there was no longer anything like departure or love of adventure. I felt protected, enveloped by motherliness, was in peace. The hallucinations were no longer exciting, but instead mild and attenuated. Somewhat later I had the feeling of possessing the same motherly strength. I perceived an inclination, a desire to help, and behaved then in an exaggeratedly sentimental and trashy manner, where medical ethics are concerned. I realized this and was able to stop.

But the depressed state of mind remained. I tried again and again to see bright and joyful images. But to no avail; only dark blue and green patterns emerged. I longed to imagine bright fire as in the first dark experiment. And I did see fires; however, they were sacrificial fires on the gloomy battlement of a citadel on a remote, autumnal heath. Once I managed to behold a bright ascending multitude of sparks, but at half-altitude it transformed itself into a group of silently moving spots from a peacock's tail. During the experiment I was very impressed that my state of mind and the type of hallucinations harmonized so consistently and uninterruptedly.

During the second dark experiment I observed that random noises, and also noises intentionally produced by the supervisor of the experiment, provoked simultaneous changes in the optical impressions (synesthesia). In the same manner, pressure on the eyeball produced alterations of visual perceptions.

Toward the end of the second dark experiment, I began to watch for sexual fantasies, which were, however, totally absent. In no way could I experience sexual desire. I wanted to imagine a picture of a woman; only a crude modern-primitive sculpture appeared. It seemed completely unerotic, and its forms were immediately replaced by agitated circles and loops

After the second dark experiment I felt benumbed and physically unwell. I perspired, was exhausted. I was thankful not to have to go to the cafeteria for lunch. The laboratory assistant who brought us the food appeared to me small and distant, of the same remarkable daintiness as the supervisor of the experiment.

Sometime around 3:00 P.M. I felt better, so that the supervisor could pursue his work. With some effort I managed to take notes myself. I sat at the table, wanted to read, but could not concentrate. Once I seemed to myself like a shape from a surrealistic picture, whose limbs were not connected with the body, but were rather painted somewhere close by...

I was depressed and thought with interest of the possibility of suicide. With some terror I apprehended that such thoughts were remarkably familiar to me. It seemed

*singularly self-evident that a depressed person commits
suicide...*

*On the way home and in the evening I was again
euphoric, brimming with the experiences of the morning. I
had experienced unexpected, impressive things. It seemed to
me that a great epoch of my life had been crowded into a few
hours. I was tempted to repeat the experiment.*

*The next day I was careless in my thinking and
conduct, had great trouble concentrating, was apathetic.... .
The casual, slightly dream-like condition persisted into the
afternoon. I had great trouble reporting in any organized
way on a simple problem. I felt a growing general weariness,
an increasing awareness that I had now returned to
everyday reality.*

*The second day after the experiment brought an
irresolute state... Mild, but distinct depression was
experienced during the following week, a feeling which of
course could be related only indirectly to LSD.*

THE PSYCHIC EFFECTS OF LSD

The picture of the activity of LSD obtained from these first
investigations was not new to science. It largely matched the
commonly held view of mescaline, an alkaloid that had been
investigated as early as the turn of the century. Mescaline is
the psychoactive constituent of a Mexican cactus *Lophophora
williamsii* (syn. *Anhalonium lewinii*). This cactus has been eaten
by American Indians ever since pre-Columbian times, and is
still used today as a sacred drug in religious ceremonies. In his
monograph *Phantastica* (Verlag Georg Stilke, Berlin, 1924), has
amply described the history of this drug, called *peyotl* by the
Aztecs. The alkaloid mescaline was isolated from the cactus by A.
Heffter in 1896, and in 1919 its chemical structure was elucidated
and it was produced synthetically by E. Spath. It was the first
hallucinogen or phantasticum (as this type of active compound

was described by Lewin to become available as a pure substance, permitting the study of chemically induced changes of sensory perceptions, mental illusions (hallucinations), and alterations of consciousness. In the 1920s extended experiments with mescaline were carried out on animal and human subjects and described comprehensively by K. Beringer in his book *Der Meskalinrausch* (Verlag Julius Springer, Berlin, 1927). Because these investigations failed to indicate any applications of mescaline in medicine, interest in this active substance waned.

With the discovery of LSD, hallucinogen research received a new impetus. The novelty of LSD as opposed to mescaline was its high activity, lying in a different order of magnitude. The active dose of mescaline, 0.2 to 0.5 g, is comparable to 0.00002 to 0.0001 g of LSD; in other words, LSD is some 5,000 to 10,000 times more active than mescaline.

LSD's unique position among the psychopharmaceuticals is not only due to its high activity, in a quantitative sense. The substance also has qualitative significance: it manifests a high specificity, that is, an activity aimed specifically at the human psyche. It can be assumed, therefore, that LSD affects the highest control centers of the psychic and intellectual functions.

The psychic effects of LSD, which are produced by such minimal quantities of material, are too meaningful and too multiform to be explained by toxic alterations of brain function. If LSD acted only through a toxic effect on the brain, then LSD experiences would be entirely psychopathological in meaning, without any psychological or psychiatric interest. On the contrary, it is likely that alterations of nerve conductivity and influence on the activity of nerve connections (synapses), which have been experimentally demonstrated, play an important role. This could mean that an influence is being exerted on the extremely complex system of cross-connections and synapses between the many billions of brain cells, the system on which the higher psychic and intellectual functions depend. This would be a promising area to explore in the search for an explanation of LSD's radical efficacy.

The nature of LSD's activity could lead to numerous possibilities of medicinal-psychiatric uses, as W. A. Stoll's ground-breaking studies had already shown. Sandoz therefore made the new active substance available to research institutes and physicians as an experimental drug, giving it the trade name Delysid (D-Lysergsaure-diathylamid) which I had proposed. The printed prospectus below describes possible applications of this kind and voices the necessary precautions.

DELYSID (LSD 25)
D-lysergic acid diethylamide tartrate
Sugar-coated tablets containing 0.025 mg (25 mcg).
Ampules of 1 mL containing 0.1 mg (100 mcg) for oral administration.

The solution may also be injected SC or IV. The effect is identical with that of oral administration but sets in more rapidly.

PROPERTIES
The administration of very small doses of Delysid (1/2-2 mcg/kg body weight) results in transitory disturbances of affect, hallucinations, depersonalization, reliving of repressed memories, and mild neurovegetative symptoms. The effect sets in after 30 to 90 minutes and generally lasts 5 to 12 hours. However, intermittent disturbances of affect may occasionally persist for several days.

METHOD OF ADMINISTRATION
For oral administration the contents of 1 ampule of Delysid are diluted with distilled water, a 1% solution of tartaric acid or halogen-free tap water.

The absorption of the solution is somewhat more rapid and more constant than that of the tablets.

Ampules which have not been opened, which have been protected against light and stored in a cool place are stable

for an unlimited period. Ampules which have been opened
or diluted solutions retain their effectiveness for 1 to 2 days,
if stored in a refrigerator.

INDICATIONS AND DOSAGE

a) Analytical psychotherapy, to elicit release of repressed
material and provide mental relaxation, particularly in
anxiety states and obsessional neuroses.

The initial dose is 25 mcg (1/4 of an ampule or 1 tablet).
This dose is increased at each treatment by 25 mcg until the
optimum dose (usually between 50 and 200 mcg) is found.
The individual treatments are best given at intervals of one
week.

b) Experimental studies on the nature of psychoses: By
taking Delysid himself, the psychiatrist is able to gain an
insight into the world of ideas and sensations of mental
patients. Delysid can also be used to induce model psychoses
of short duration in normal subjects, thus facilitating studies
on the pathogenesis of mental disease.

In normal subjects, doses of 25 to 75 mcg are generally
sufficient to produce a hallucinatory psychosis (on an
average 1 mcg/kg body weight). In certain forms of
psychosis and in chronic alcoholism, higher doses are
necessary (2 to 4 mcg/kg body weight).

PRECAUTIONS

Pathological mental conditions may be intensified by
Delysid. Particular caution is necessary in subjects with
a suicidal tendency and in those cases where a psychotic
development appears imminent. The psycho-affective
liability and the tendency to commit impulsive acts may
occasionally last for some days.

Delysid should only be administered under strict medical
supervision. The supervision should not be discontinued
until the effects of the drug have completely worn off.

ANTIDOTE
The mental effects of Delysid can be rapidly reversed by
the i.m. administration of 50 mg. chlorpromazine.

LITERATURE AVAILABLE ON REQUEST.
Sandoz Ltd., Basel, Switzerland

The use of LSD in analytical psychotherapy is based mainly on
the following psychic effects.

In LSD inebriation the accustomed worldview undergoes
a deep-seated transformation and disintegration. Connected
with this is a loosening or even suspension of the I-you barrier.
Patients who are bogged down in an egocentric problem cycle can
thereby be helped to release themselves from their fixation and
isolation. The result can be an improved rapport with the doctor
and a greater susceptibility to psychotherapeutic influence. The
enhanced suggestibility under the influence of LSD works toward
the same goal.

Another significant, psychotherapeutically valuable
characteristic of LSD inebriation is the tendency of long
forgotten or suppressed contents of experience to appear
again in consciousness. Traumatic events, which are sought in
psychoanalysis, may then become accessible to psychotherapeutic
treatment. Numerous case histories tell of experiences from
even the earliest childhood that were vividly recalled during
psychoanalysis under the influence of LSD. This does not
involve an ordinary recollection, but rather a true reliving; not a
reminiscence, but rather a reviviscence, as the French psychiatrist
Jean Delay has formulated it.

LSD does not act as a true medicament; rather it plays
the role of a drug aid in the context of psychoanalytic and
psychotherapeutic treatment and serves to channel the treatment
more effectively and to shorten its duration. It can fulfill this
function in two particular ways.

In one procedure, which was developed in European clinics and given the name psycholytic therapy, moderately strong doses of LSD are administered in several successive sessions at regular intervals. Subsequently the LSD experiences are worked out in group discussions, and in expression therapy by drawing and painting. The term psycholytic therapy was coined by Ronald A. Sandison, an English therapist of Jungian Orientation and a pioneer of clinical LSD research. The root -lysis or -lytic signifies the dissolution of tension or conflicts in the human psyche.

In a second procedure, which is the favored treatment in the United States, a single, very high LSD dose (0.3 to 0.6 mg) is administered after correspondingly intensive psychological preparation of the patients. This method, described as psychedelic therapy, attempts to induce a mystical-religious experience through the shock effects of LSD. This experience can then serve as a starting point for a restructuring and curing of the patient's personality in the accompanying psychotherapeutic treatment. The term psychedelic, which can be translated as "mind-manifesting" or "mind-expanding," was introduced by Humphry Osmond, a pioneer of LSD research in the United States.

LSD's apparent benefits as a drug auxiliary in psychoanalysis and psychotherapy are derived from properties diametrically opposed to the effects of tranquilizer-type psychopharmaceuticals. Whereas tranquilizers tend to cover up the patient's problems and conflicts, reducing their apparent gravity and importance, LSD makes them more exposed and more intensely experienced. This clearer recognition of problems and conflicts makes them, in turn, more susceptible to psychotherapeutic treatment.

The suitability and success of LSD in psychoanalysis and psychotherapy are still a subject of controversy in professional circles. The same could be said, however, of other procedures employed in psychiatry such as electroshock, insulin therapy, or psychosurgery, procedures that entail, moreover, a far greater risk than the use of LSD, which under suitable conditions can be considered practically safe.

Because forgotten or repressed experiences, under the influence of LSD, may become conscious with considerable speed, the treatment can be correspondingly shortened. To some psychiatrists, however, this reduction of the therapy's duration is a disadvantage. They are of the opinion that this precipitation leaves the patient insufficient time for psychotherapeutic working-through. The therapeutic effect, they believe, persists for a shorter time than when there is a gradual treatment, including a slow process of becoming conscious of the traumatic experiences.

Psycholytic and especially psychedelic therapy require thorough preparation of the patient for the LSD experience, to avoid his or her being frightened by the unusual and the unfamiliar. Only then is a positive interpretation of the experience possible. The selection of patients is also important, since not all types of psychic disturbance respond equally well to these methods of treatment. Successful use of LSD-assisted psychoanalysis and psychotherapy presupposes specific knowledge and experience.

In this respect, self-examination by psychiatrists, as W. A. Stoll has pointed out, can be most useful. They provide the doctors with direct insight, based on first-hand experience into the strange world of LSD inebriation, and make it possible for them truly to understand these phenomena in their patients, to interpret them properly, and to take full advantage of them.

The following pioneers in use of LSD as a drug aid in psychoanalysis and psychotherapy deserve to be named in the front rank: A. K. Busch and W. C. Johnson, S. Cohen and, H. A. Abramson, H. Osmond, and A. Hoffer in the United States; R. A. Sandison in England; W. Frederking and H. Leuner in Germany; and G. Roubicek and S. Grof in Czechoslovakia.

The second indication for LSD cited in the Sandoz prospectus on Delysid concerns its use in experimental investigations on the nature of psychoses. This arises from the fact that extraordinary psychic states experimentally produced by LSD in healthy research subjects are similar to many manifestations of certain mental disturbances. In the early days of LSD research, it was often claimed that LSD inebriation has something to do with a type of "model psychosis." This idea was dismissed, however, because extended comparative investigations showed that there were essential differences between the manifestations of psychosis and the LSD experience. With the LSD model, nevertheless, it is possible to study deviations from the normal psychic and mental condition, and to observe the biochemical and electrophysiological alterations associated with them. Perhaps we shall thereby gain new insights into the nature of psychoses. According to certain theories, various mental disturbances could be produced by psychotoxic metabolic products that have the power, even in minimal quantities, to alter the functions of brain cells. LSD represents a substance that certainly does not occur in the human organism, but whose existence and activity let it seem possible that abnormal metabolic products could exist, that even in trace quantities could produce mental disturbances. As a result, the conception of a biochemical origin of certain mental disturbances has received broader support, and research in this direction has been stimulated.

One medicinal use of LSD that touches on fundamental ethical questions is its administration to the dying. This practice arose from observations in American clinics that especially severe painful conditions of cancer patients, which no longer respond to conventional pain-relieving medication, could be alleviated or completely abolished by LSD. Of course, this does not involve an analgesic effect in the true sense. The diminution of pain sensitivity may rather occur because patients under the influence of LSD are psychologically so dissociated from their bodies that physical pain no longer penetrates their consciousness. In order for LSD to be effective in such cases, it is especially crucial that patients be prepared and instructed about the kind of experiences and transformations that await them. In many cases it has proved beneficial for either a member of the clergy or a psychotherapist to guide the patient's thoughts in a religious direction. Numerous case histories tell of patients who gained meaningful insights about life and death on their deathbeds as, freed from pain in LSD ecstasy and reconciled to their fate, they faced their earthly demise fearlessly and in peace.

The hitherto existing knowledge about the administration of LSD to the terminally ill has been summarized and published by S. Grof and J. Halifax in their book *The Human Encounter with Death* (E. P. Dutton, New York, 1977). The authors, together with E. Kast, S. Cohen, and W. A. Pahnke, are among the pioneers of this application of LSD.

The most recent comprehensive publication on the use of LSD in psychiatry, *Realms of the Human Unconscious: Observations from LSD Research* (The Viking Press, New York, 1975), likewise comes from the Czech psychiatrist who has emigrated to the United States. This book offers a critical evaluation of the LSD experience from the viewpoint of Freud and Jung, as well as of existential analysis.

Chapter 5
From Remedy to Inebriant

DURING the first years after its discovery, LSD brought me the same happiness and gratification that any pharmaceutical chemist would feel on learning that a substance he or she produced might possibly develop into a valuable medicament. For the creation of new remedies is the goal of a pharmaceutical chemist's research activity; therein lies the meaning of his or her work.

NONMEDICAL USE OF LSD

This joy at having fathered LSD was tarnished after more than ten years of uninterrupted scientific research and medicinal use when LSD was swept up in the huge wave of an inebriant mania that began to spread over the Western world, above all the United States, at the end of the 1950s. It was strange how rapidly LSD adopted its new role as inebriant and, for a time, became the number-one inebriating drug, at least as far as publicity was concerned. The more its use as an inebriant was disseminated, bringing an upsurge in the number of untoward incidents caused by careless, medically unsupervised use, the more LSD became a problem child for me and for the Sandoz firm.

It was obvious that a substance with such fantastic effects on mental perception and on the experience of the outer and inner world would also arouse interest outside medical science, but I had not expected that LSD, with its unfathomably uncanny, profound effects, so unlike the character of a recreational drug, would ever find worldwide use as an inebriant. I had expected curiosity and interest on the part of artists outside of medicine—

performers, painters, and writers—but not among people in general. After the scientific publications around the turn of the century on mescaline—which, as already mentioned, evokes psychic effects quite like those of LSD—the use of this compound remained confined to medicine and to experiments within artistic and literary circles. I had expected the same fate for LSD. And indeed, the first non-medicinal self-experiments with LSD were carried out by writers, painters, musicians, and other intellectuals.

LSD sessions had reportedly provoked extraordinary aesthetic experiences and granted new insights into the essence of the creative process. Artists were influenced in their creative work in unconventional ways. A particular type of art developed that has become known as psychedelic art. It comprises creations produced under the influenced of LSD and other psychedelic drugs, whereby the drugs acted as stimulus and source of inspiration. The standard publication in this field is the book by Robert E. L. Masters and Jean Houston, *Psychedelic Art* (Balance House, 1968). Works of psychedelic art are not created while the drug is in effect, but only afterward, the artist being inspired by these experiences. As long as the inebriated condition lasts, creative activity is impeded, if not completely halted. The influx of images is too great and is increasing too rapidly to be portrayed and fashioned. An overwhelming vision paralyzes activity. Artistic productions arising directly from LSD inebriation, therefore, are mostly rudimentary in character and deserve consideration not because of their artistic merit, but because they are a type of psychoprogram, which offers insight into the deepest mental structures of the artist, activated and made conscious by LSD. This was demonstrated later in a large-scale experiment by the Munich psychiatrist Richard P. Hartmann, in which thirty famous painters took part. He published the results in his book *Mlerei aus Bereichen des Unbewussten: Kunstler Experimentieren unter LSD* [Painting from spheres of the unconscious: artists experiment with LSD], Verlag M. Du Mont Schauberg, Cologne, 1974).

LSD experiments also gave new impetus to exploration into the essence of religious and mystical experience. Religious scholars and philosophers discussed the question whether the religious and mystical experiences often discovered in LSD sessions were genuine, that is, comparable to spontaneous mysticoreligious enlightenment.

This nonmedicinal yet earnest phase of LSD research, at times in parallel with medicinal research, at times following it, was increasingly overshadowed at the beginning of the 1960s, as LSD use spread with epidemic-like speed through all social classes, as a sensational inebriating drug, in the course of the inebriant mania in the United States. The rapid rise of drug use, which had its beginning in this country about twenty years ago, was not, however, a consequence of the discovery of LSD, as superficial observers often declared. Rather it had deep-seated sociological causes: materialism, alienation from nature through industrialization and increasing urbanization, lack of satisfaction in professional employment in a mechanized, lifeless working world, ennui and purposelessness in a wealthy, saturated society, and lack of a religious, nurturing, and meaningful philosophical foundation of life.

The existence of LSD was even regarded by the drug enthusiasts as a predestined coincidence—it had to be discovered precisely at this time in order to bring help to people suffering under the modern conditions. It is not surprising that LSD first came into circulation as an inebriating drug in the United States, the country in which industrialization, urbanization, and mechanization, even of agriculture, are most broadly advanced. These are the same factors that have led to the origin and growth of the hippie movement that developed simultaneously with the LSD wave. The two cannot be dissociated. It would be worth investigating to what extent the consumption of psychedelic drugs furthered the hippie movement and conversely.

The spread of LSD from medicine and psychiatry into the

drug scene was introduced and expedited by publications on sensational LSD experiments that, although they were carried out in psychiatric clinics and universities, were not then reported in scientific journals, but rather in magazines and daily papers, greatly elaborated. Reporters made themselves available as guinea pigs. Sidney Katz, for example, participated in an LSD experiment in the Saskatchewan Hospital in Canada under the supervision of noted psychiatrists; his experiences, however, were not published in a medical journal. Instead, he described them in an article entitled "My Twelve Hours as a Madman" in his magazine *MacLean's* ("Canada's National Magazine"), colorfully illustrated in fanciful fullness of detail. The widely distributed German magazine *Quick*, in its issue number 12 of 21 March 1954, reported a sensational eyewitness account on "Ein kuhnes wissenschaftliches Experiment" [a daring scientific experiment] by the painter Wilfried Zeller, who took "a few drops of lysergic acid" in the Viennese University Psychiatric Clinic. Of the numerous publications of this type that have made effective lay propaganda for LSD, it is sufficient to cite just one more example: a large-scale, illustrated article in *Look* magazine of September 1959. Entitled "The Curious Story Behind the New Cary Grant," it must have contributed enormously to the diffusion of LSD consumption. The famous movie star had received LSD in a respected clinic in California, in the course of a psychotherapeutic treatment. He informed the *Look* reporter that he had sought inner peace his whole life long, but yoga, hypnosis, and mysticism had not helped him. Only the treatment with LSD had made a new, self-strengthened man out of him, so that after three frustrating marriages he now believed himself really able to love and make a woman happy.

The evolution of LSD from remedy to inebriating drug was, however, primarily promoted by the activities of Dr. Timothy Leary and Dr. Richard Alpert of Harvard University. In a later section I will come to speak in more detail about Dr. Leary and my meetings with this personage who has become known worldwide as an apostle of LSD.

Books also appeared on the U.S. market in which the fantastic effects of LSD were reported more fully. Here only two of the most important will be mentioned: *Exploring Inner Space* by Jane Dunlap (Harcourt Brace and World, New York, 1961) and *My Self and I* by Constance A. Newland (N A.L. Signet Books, New York, 1963). Although in both cases LSD was used within the scope of a psychiatric treatment, the authors addressed their books, which became bestsellers, to the broad public. In her book, subtitled "The Intimate and Completely Frank Record of One Woman's Courageous Experiment with Psychiatry's Newest Drug, LSD 25," Constance A. Newland described in intimate detail how she had been cured of frigidity. After such avowals, one can easily imagine that many people would want to try the wondrous medicine for themselves. The mistaken opinion created by such reports—that it would be sufficient simply to take LSD in order to accomplish such miraculous effects and transformations in oneself—soon led to broad diffusion of self-experimentation with the new drug.

Objective, informative books about LSD and its problems also appeared, such as the excellent work by the psychiatrist Dr. Sidney Cohen, *The Beyond Within* (Atheneum, New York, 1967), in which the dangers of careless use are clearly exposed. This had, however, no power to put a stop to the LSD epidemic.

As LSD experiments were often carried out in ignorance of the uncanny, unforeseeable, profound effects, and without medical supervision, they frequently came to a bad end. With increasing LSD consumption in the drug scene, there came an increase in "horror trips"—LSD experiments that led to disoriented conditions and panic, often resulting in accidents and even crime.

The rapid rise of nonmedicinal LSD consumption at the beginning of the 1960s was also partly attributable to the fact that the drug laws then current in most countries did not include LSD. For this reason, drug users changed from the legally proscribed narcotics to the still-legal substance LSD. Moreover, the last of the Sandoz patents for the production of LSD expired in 1963, removing a further hindrance to illegal manufacture of the drug.

The rise of LSD in the drug scene caused our firm a nonproductive, laborious burden. National control laboratories and health authorities requested statements from us about chemical and pharmacological properties, stability and toxicity of LSD, and analytical methods for its detection in confiscated drug samples, as well as in the human body, in blood and urine. This brought a voluminous correspondence, which expanded in connection with inquiries from all over the world about accidents, poisonings, criminal acts, and so forth, resulting from misuse of LSD. All this meant enormous, unprofitable difficulties, which the business management of Sandoz regarded with disapproval. Thus it happened one day that Professor Stoll, managing director of the firm at the time, said to me reproachfully: "I would rather you had not discovered LSD."

At that time, I was now and again assailed by doubts whether the valuable pharmacological and psychic effects of LSD might be outweighed by its dangers and by possible injuries due to misuse. Would LSD become a blessing for humanity, or a curse? This I often asked myself when I thought about my problem child. My other preparations, Methergine, Dihydroergotamine, and Hydergine, caused me no such problems and difficulties. They were not problem children; lacking extravagant properties leading to misuse, they have developed in a satisfying manner into therapeutically valuable medicines.

The publicity about LSD attained its high point in the years 1964 to 1966, not only with regard to enthusiastic claims about the wondrous effects of LSD by drug fanatics and hippies, but also to reports of accidents, mental breakdowns, criminal acts, murders, and suicide under the influence of LSD. A veritable LSD hysteria reigned.

SANDOZ STOPS LSD DISTRIBUTION

In view of this situation, the management of Sandoz was forced to make a public statement on the LSD problem and to publish accounts of the corresponding measures that had been taken. The pertinent letter, dated 23 August 1965, by Dr. A. Cerletti, at the time director of the Pharmaceutical Department of Sandoz, is reproduced below:

DECISION REGARDING LSD 25
AND OTHER HALLUCINOGENIC SUBSTANCES

More than twenty years have elapsed since the discovery by Albert Hofmann of LSD 25 in the SANDOZ Laboratories. Whereas the fundamental importance of this discovery may be assessed by its impact on the development of modern psychiatric research, it must be recognized that it placed a heavy burden of responsibility on SANDOZ, the owner of this product.

The finding of a new chemical with outstanding biological properties, apart from the scientific interest implied by its synthesis, is usually the first decisive step toward profitable development of a new drug. In the case of LSD, however, it soon became clear that, despite the outstanding properties of this compound, or rather because of the very nature of these qualities, even though LSD was fully protected by SANDOZ-owned patents since the time of its first synthesis in 1938, the usual means of practical exploitation could not be envisaged.

On the other hand, all the evidence obtained following the initial studies in animals and humans carried out in the SANDOZ research laboratories pointed to the important role that this substance could play as an investigational tool in neurological research and in psychiatry.

It was therefore decided to make LSD available free of charge to qualified experimental and clinical investigators all over the world. This broad research approach was assisted by the provision of any necessary technical aid and in many instances also by financial support.

An enormous amount of scientific documents, published mainly in the international biochemical and medical literature and systematically listed in the "SANDOZ Bibliography on LSD" as well as in the "Catalogue of Literature on Delysid" periodically edited by SANDOZ, gives vivid proof of what has been achieved by following this line of policy over nearly two decades. By exercising this kind of "nobile officium" in accordance with the highest standards of medical ethics with all kinds of self-imposed precautions and restrictions, it was possible for many years to avoid the danger of abuse (i.e., use by people neither competent nor qualified), which is always inherent in a compound with exceptional CNS activity.

In spite of all our precautions, cases of LSD abuse have occurred from time to time in varying circumstances completely beyond the control of SANDOZ. Very recently this danger has increased considerably and in some parts of the world has reached the scale of a serious threat to public health. This state of affairs has now reached a critical point for the following reasons: (1) A worldwide spread of misconceptions of LSD has been caused by an increasing amount of publicity aimed at provoking an active interest in laypeople by means of sensational stories and statements; (2) In most countries no adequate legislation exists to control and regulate the production and distribution of substances like LSD; (3) The problem of availability of LSD, once limited on technical grounds, has fundamentally changed with the advent of mass production of lysergic acid by fermentation procedures. Since the last patent on LSD expired in 1963, it is not surprising to find that an increasing number of dealers in fine chemicals are offering LSD from unknown sources at the high price known to be paid by LSD fanatics.

Taking into consideration all the above-mentioned circumstances and the flood of requests for LSD which has now become uncontrollable, the pharmaceutical

management of SANDOZ has decided to stop immediately
all further production and distribution of LSD. The same
policy will apply to all derivatives or analogues of LSD with
hallucinogenic properties as well as to Psilocybin, Psilocin,
and their hallucinogenic congeners.

For a while the distribution of LSD and psilocybin was
stopped completely by Sandoz. Most countries had subsequently
proclaimed strict regulations concerning possession, distribution,
and use of hallucinogens, so that physicians, psychiatric clinics,
and research institutes, if they could produce a special permit to
work with these substances from the respective national health
authorities, could again be supplied with LSD and psilocybin.
In the United States the National Institute of Mental Health
(NIMH) undertook the distribution of these agents to licensed
research institutes.

All these legislative and official precautions, however, had little
influence on LSD consumption in the drug scene, yet on the other
hand hindered and continue to hinder medicinal-psychiatric
use and LSD research in biology and neurology, because many
researchers dread the red tape that is connected with the
procurement of a license for the use of LSD. The bad reputation
of LSD—its depiction as an "insanity drug" and a "satanic
invention"—constitutes a further reason why many doctors
shunned use of LSD in their psychiatric practice.

In the course of recent years the uproar of publicity about LSD
has quieted, and the consumption of LSD as an inebriant has also
diminished, as far as that can be concluded from the rare reports
about accidents and other regrettable occurrences following LSD
ingestion. It may be that the decrease of LSD accidents, however,
is not simply due to a decline in LSD consumption. Possibly the
recreational users, with time, have become more aware of the
particular effects and dangers of LSD and more cautious in their
use of this drug. Certainly LSD, which was for a time considered

in the Western world, above all in the United States, to be the number-one inebriant, has relinquished this leading role to other inebriants such as hashish and the habituating, even physically destructive drugs like heroin and amphetamine. The last-mentioned drugs represent an alarrning sociological and public health problem today.

Dangers of Nonmedicinal LSD Experiments

While professional use of LSD in psychiatry entails hardly any risk, the ingestion of this substance outside of medical practice, without medical supervision, is subject to multifarious dangers. These dangers reside, on the one hand, in external circumstances connected with illegal drug use and, on the other hand, in the peculiarity of LSD's psychic effects.

The advocates of uncontrolled, free use of LSD and other hallucinogens base their attitude on two claims: (l) this type of drug produces no addiction, and (2) until now no danger to health from moderate use of hallucinogens has been demonstrated. Both are true. Genuine addiction, characterized by the fact that psychic and often severe physical disturbances appear on withdrawal of the drug, has not been observed, even in cases in which LSD was taken often and over a long period of time. No organic injury or death as a direct consequence of an LSD intoxication has yet been reported. As discussed in greater detail in the chapter "LSD in Animal Experiments and Biological Research," LSD is actually a relatively nontoxic substance in proportion to its extraordinarily high psychic activity.

Psychotic Reactions

Like the other hallucinogens, however, LSD is dangerous in an entirely different sense. While the psychic and physical dangers of the addicting narcotics, the opiates, amphetamines, and so forth, appear only with chronic use, the possible danger of LSD exists in every single experiment. This is because severe

Rye infected with ergot.
Courtesy of The Canadian Phytopathologicial Society.
From *Diseases of Field Crops in Canada.* 2003.
Eds. K.I Bailey, B.D. Gossen, R.K. Gugel and
R.A.A. Morrall. The Canadian Phytopathological
Society, Saskatoon, SK.

Woodcut of St. Anthony, the patron
saint of ergotism victims. Ergot poisoning
was originally known as St. Anthony's Fire.
Courtesy of the Staatliche Graphische Sammlung
München.

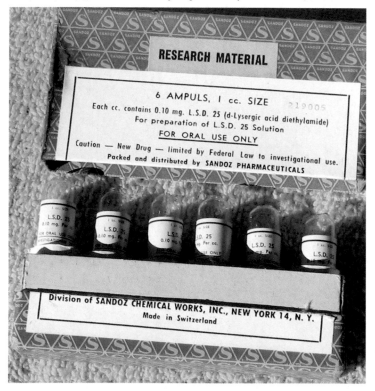

Dr. Hofmann's lab notes. An excerpt from the author's journal concerning the preparation of LSD tartrate and the first planned self-experiment.
Courtesy of the author.

Sandoz LSD. Sandoz made LSD available to research institutes and physicians as an experimental drug, giving it the trade name *Delysid*.
Anonymous photographer, © 2005 Erowid.org. Image colorized by Yumi Uno Mundo, 2005.

**Dr. Hofmann and
the LSD-25 molecule.**
Courtesy of the author.

The Hofmann Collection.
Originally compiled by the Sandoz
staff, the nearly 4,000 research
papers on LSD and psilocybin in
the Hofmann Collection are now
available in an online database.
(See the appendix on p. 211
for more information.)
Image by Fire Erowid, © 2002 Erowid.org.
Image colorized by Yumi Uno Mundo, 2005.

Drop Acid Not Bombs. "The existence of LSD was even regarded by the drug enthusiasts as a predestined coincidence–it has to be discovered precisely at this time
in order to bring help to people suffering under the modern conditions" (p. 81). LSD
was discovered in 1943; the atomic bomb was developed between 1942 and 1945.
Photo by Robert Altman, © Robert Altman (www.altmanphoto.com).

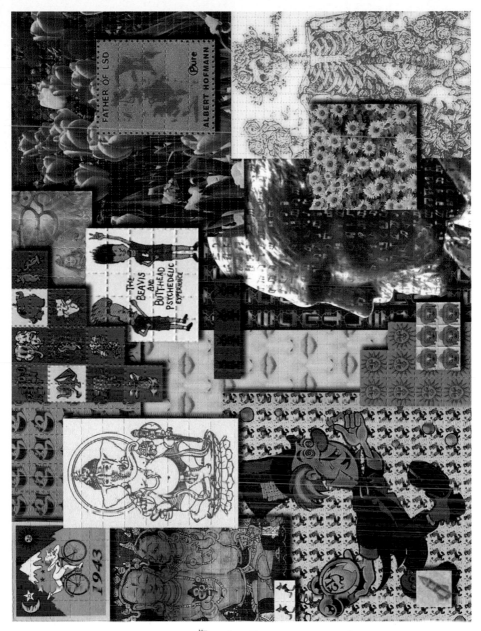

LSD blotter paper.

Black market LSD is often sold on perforated blotter paper, the design of which has become an elaborate underground art form. Note the bicyclist in the upper left, a portrayal of Dr. Hofmann's ride home during the first planned self-experiment with LSD (p. 48). Other images shown here reference popular culture, salute Timothy Leary, and invoke religious themes.

Image by Fire Erowid,
© 2005 Erowid.org.

The hippies' hero. A caricature of the author adorned with
the symbols of 1960s psychedelia. Drawing by Bouyum, 1970.

Portrait of Dr. Hofmann in his home.

Image by
Dean Chamberlain,
© Dean Chamberlain,
all rights reserved

Aldous and Laura Huxley. Author of *Brave New World* and *Island,* Aldous Huxley was one of the most articulate advocates of LSD's potential. Courtesy of Laura Archera Huxley.

Stanislav Grof, M.D. A pioneering LSD psychotherapist who emigrated to the United States from Czechoslovakia, Dr. Grof was among the first to study the effects of LSD psychotherapy on the terminally ill. Photo by Kent Martin, producer of *Hofmann's Potion* (2002).

Timothy Leary and Richard Alpert. "Shortly thereafter, Leary and Alpert were discharged from the teaching staff of Harvard University because the investigations, at first conducted in an academic milieu, had lost their scientific character" (p. 96). Origin unknown.

Albert Hofmann and Timothy Leary. "The greeting was cordial, a symbol of our fateful relationship through LSD"(p. 98). Courtesy of the author.

October 2005. Tav Sparks, Stanislav Grof, Albert Hofmann, H. R. Giger, and Carmen Scheifele. The H. R. Giger Museum in Gruyere, Switzerland. Photograph by Wolfgang Holz.

Mushroom stones. Two views of a pre-Columbian stone mushroom icon from classic Mayan culture (circa 300-600 A.D.). From the collection of the Rietberg Museum, Zurich.

Aztec mushroom eater. This detail from a 17th-century Aztec codex shows the death god *Mictlantecuhtli* with a person eating a sacred mushroom. *Codex Magliabecchi, Mexico.* From *Plants of the Gods,* 1979. R. Shultes and A. Hofmann, McGraw Hill, New York, p. 216.

Artificially cultivated *psilocybe mexicana*. One of about a dozen different species of psychoactive mushrooms used ceremonially by the Mazatecs, and botanically identified by Roger Heim, who accompanied the Wassons on their expeditions. Photo courtesy of Sporeworks, © Sporeworks.com.

***Ipomoea violacea*.** This is the most common morning glory, and its seeds are used ceremonially by the Zapotec people along with the seeds of *Rivea (Turbina) corymbosa*. Both plants contain lysergic acid amide, or LSA. Photo by F. Conte, © 2001 Erowid.org.

R. Gordon and Valentina Pavlovna Wasson. The Wassons' expeditions to the mountains of southern Mexico brought the knowledge of psychoactive mushrooms to industrialized society.
Photo archives of Gordon and Valentina Wasson, with thanks to Robert Forte.

Maria Sabina. "How should we judge the conduct of Maria Sabina, the fact that she allowed strangers, white people, access to the secret ceremony, and let them try the sacred mushrooms?" (p. 152). Photo archives of Gordon and Valentina Wasson, with thanks to Robert Forte.

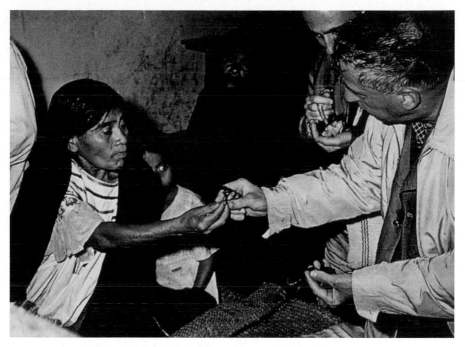

Gordon Wasson and Maria Sabina. "Wasson describes how the mushroom seized possession of him completely, although he had tried to struggle against its effects, in order to be able to remain an objective observer" (p. 124).
Photo archives of Gordon and Valentina Wasson, with thanks to Robert Forte.

Historical illustration of ololiuhqui.
The earliest account of *Rivea corymbosa* (also known as *Turbina corymbosa*), the sacred morning glory.
From Francisco Hernandez's *Rerum Medicarum Novae Hispaniae Thesaurus seu Plantarum, Animalium, Mineralium Mexicanorum Historia*, published in Rome in 1651.

De OLILIVHQVI, seu planta orbicularium foliorum. Cap. XIV.

OLILIVHQVI, quam *Coaxihuitl*, seu herbam Serpentis alij vocant, volubilis herba eft, folia viridia ferens, tenuia,cordis figura. caules teretes,virides,tenuefq;. flores albos, & longiufculos. femen rotundum fimile Coriandro,vnde nomen. radices fibris fimiles, calida quarto ordine planta eft. luem Gallicam curat. dolores è frigore ortos fedat. flatum, ac præter naturam rumores difcutit. puluis refina mixtus pellit frigus. luxatis aut fractis offibus, & lumbis fœminarum laxis,aucto robore mirum auxiliatur in modum.S eminis etiam, eft vfus in medicina, quod tritum,ac deuoratum, illitumq; capiti, & fronti, cum lacte & *Chilli*, fertur morbis oculorum mederi. deuoratum verò, venerem excitat. Acri eft fapore, & temperie, veluti & planta eius, impensè calida. Indorum facrifici cum videri volebant verfari cum Superis,ac refpófa accipere ab eis,ea vefcebátur planta,vt defiperent, milleq; phantafmata,& dæmonú obuerfátium effigies circumfpectarent. qua in re Solano maniaco Diofcoridis fimilis fortaffe alicui videri poffit.

Albert Hofmann, 2002.
Photo by Kent Martin, producer of *Hofmann's Potion* (2002).

Portrait of the author.
Courtesy of Dr. Hofmann.

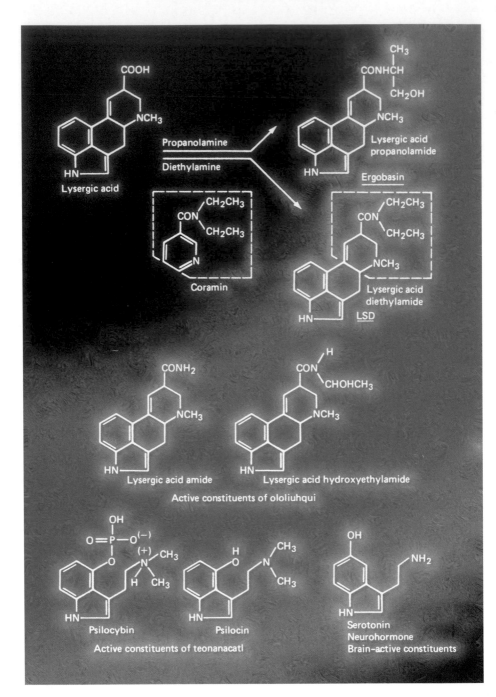

Chemical Structures.

disoriented states can appear during any LSD inebriation. It is true that through careful preparation of the experiment and the experimenter such episodes can largely be avoided, but they cannot be excluded with certainty. LSD crises resemble psychotic attacks with a manic or depressive character.

In the manic, hyperactive condition, the feeling of omnipotence or invulnerability can lead to serious casualties. Such accidents have occurred when inebriated persons confused in this way—believing themselves to be invulnerable—walked in front of a moving automobile or jumped out a window in the belief that they were able to fly. This type of LSD casualty, however, is not so common as one might be led to think on the basis of reports that were sensationally exaggerated by the mass media. Nevertheless, such reports must serve as serious warnings.

On the other hand, a report that made the rounds worldwide, in 1966, about an alleged murder committed under the influence on LSD, cannot be true. The suspect, a young man in New York accused of having killed his mother-in-law, explained at his arrest, immediately after the fact, that he knew nothing of the crime and that he had been on an LSD trip for three days. But an LSD inebriation, even with the highest doses, lasts no longer than twelve hours, and repeated ingestion leads to tolerance, which means that extra doses are ineffective. Besides, LSD inebriation is characterized by the fact that the person remembers exactly what he or she has experienced. Presumably the defendant in this case expected leniency for extenuating circumstances, owing to unsoundness of mind.

The danger of a psychotic reaction is especially great if LSD is given to someone without his or her knowledge. This was demonstrated in an episode that took place soon after the discovery of LSD, during the first investigations with the new substance in the Zurich University Psychiatric Clinic, when people were not yet aware of the danger of such jokes. A young doctor, whose colleagues had slipped LSD into his coffee as a lark, wanted to swim across Lake Zurich during the winter at -20°C (-4°F) and had to be prevented by force.

There is a different danger when the LSD-induced disorientation exhibits a depressive rather than manic character. In the course of such an LSD experiment, frightening visions, death agony, or the fear of becoming insane can lead to a threatening psychic breakdown or even to suicide. Here the LSD trip becomes a "horror trip."

The demise of a Dr. Olson, who had been given LSD without his knowledge in the course of U.S. Army drug experiments, and who then committed suicide by jumping from a window, caused a particular sensation. His family could not understand how this quiet, well-adjusted man could have been driven to this deed. Not until fifteen years later, when the secret documents about the experiments were published, did they learn the true circumstances, whereupon the president of the United States publicly apologized to the dependents. [Publisher's note: Years later, Dr. Frank Olson was revealed to be a CIA officer, and the circumstances around his death are still mysterious. For an excellent history of the CIA's involvement with LSD, see *Acid Dreams* by Martin Lee and Bruce Shlain (Grove Press, 1985).]

The conditions for the positive outcome of an LSD experiment, with little possibility of a psychotic derailment, reside on the one hand in the individual and on the other hand in the external milieu of the experiment. The internal, personal factors are called set, the external conditions setting.

The beauty of a living room or of an outdoor location is perceived with particular force because of the highly stimulated sense organs during LSD inebriation, and such an amenity has a substantial influence on the course of the experiment. The persons present, their appearance, their traits, are also part of the setting that determines the experience. The acoustic milieu is equally significant. Even harmless noises can turn to torment, and conversely lovely music can develop into a euphoric experience.

With LSD experiments in ugly or noisy surroundings, however, there is greater danger of a negative outcome, including psychotic crises. The machine- and appliance-world of today offers much scenery and all types of noise that could very well trigger panic during enhanced sensibility.

Just as meaningful as the external milieu of the LSD experience, if not even more important, is the mental condition of the experimenters, their current state of mind, their attitude to the drug experience, and their expectations associated with it. Even unconscious feelings of happiness or fear can have an effect. LSD tends to intensify the actual psychic state. A feeling of happiness can be heightened to bliss, a depression can deepen to despair. LSD is thus the most inappropriate means imaginable for curing a depressive state. It is dangerous to take LSD in a disturbed, unhappy frame of mind, or in a state of fear. The probability that the experiment will end in a psychic breakdown is then quite high.

Among persons with unstable personality structures, tending to psychotic reactions, LSD experimentation ought to be completely avoided. Here an LSD shock, by releasing a latent psychosis, can produce a lasting mental injury.

The psyche of very young persons should also be considered as unstable, in the sense of not yet having matured. In any case, the shock of such a powerful stream of new and strange perceptions and feelings, such as is engendered by LSD, endangers the sensitive, still-developing psycho-organism. Even the medicinal use of LSD in youths under eighteen years of age, in the scope of psychoanalytic or psychotherapeutic treatment, is discouraged in professional circles, correctly so in my opinion. Juveniles for the most part still lack a secure, solid relationship to reality. Such a relationship is needed before the dramatic experience of new dimensions of reality can be meaningfully integrated into the worldview. Instead of leading to a broadening and deepening of reality consciousness, such an experience in adolescents will lead to insecurity and a feeling of being lost. Because of the freshness of sensory perception in youth and the still-unlimited capacity for experience, spontaneous visionary experiences occur much more frequently than in later life. For this reason as well, psychostimulating agents should not be used by juveniles.

Even in healthy, adult persons, even with adherence to all of the preparatory and protective measures discussed, an LSD experiment can fail, causing psychotic reactions. Medical supervision is therefore earnestly to be recommended, even for nonmedicinal LSD experiments. This should include an examination of the state of health before the experiment. The doctor need not be present at the session; however, medical help should at all times be readily available.

Acute LSD psychoses can be cut short and brought under control quickly and reliably by injection of chlorpromazine or another sedative of this type.

The presence of a familiar person, who can request medical help in the event of an emergency, is also an indispensable psychological assurance. Although the LSD inebriation is characterized mostly by an immersion in the individual inner world, a deep need for human contact sometimes arises, especially in depressive phases.

LSD FROM THE BLACK MARKET

Nonmedicinal LSD consumption can bring dangers of an entirely different type than hitherto discussed: for most of the LSD offered in the drug scene is of unknown origin. LSD preparations from the black market are unreliable when it comes to both quality and dosage. They rarely contain the declared quantity, but mostly have less LSD, often none at all, and sometimes even too much. In many cases other drugs or even poisonous substances are sold as LSD. These observations were made in our laboratory upon analysis of a great number of LSD samples from the black market. They coincide with the experiences of national drug control departments.

The unreliability in the strength of LSD preparations on the illicit drug market can lead to dangerous overdosage. Overdoses have often proved to be the cause of failed LSD experiments that led to severe psychic and physical breakdowns. Reports of alleged fatal LSD poisoning, however, have yet to be confirmed. Close scrutiny of such cases invariably established other causative factors.

The following case, which took place in 1970, is cited as an example of the possible dangers of black market LSD. We received for investigation from the police a drug powder distributed as LSD. It came from a young man who was admitted to the hospital in critical condition and whose friend had also ingested this preparation and died as a result. Analysis showed that the powder contained no LSD, but rather the very poisonous alkaloid strychnine.

If most black market LSD preparations contained less than the stated quantity and often no LSD at all, the reason is either deliberate falsification or the great instability of this substance. LSD is very sensitive to air and light. It is oxidatively destroyed by the oxygen in the air and is transformed into an inactive substance under the influence of light. This must be taken into account during the synthesis and especially during the production of stable, storable forms of LSD. Claims that LSD may easily be prepared, or that every chemistry student in a half-decent laboratory is capable of producing it, are untrue. Procedures for synthesis of LSD have indeed been published and are accessible to everyone. With these detailed procedures in hand, chemists would be able to carry out the synthesis, provided they had pure lysergic acid at their disposal; its possession today, however, is subject to the same strict regulations as LSD. In order to isolate LSD in pure crystalline form from the reaction solution and in order to produce stable preparations, however, special equipment and not easily acquired specific experience are required, owing (as stated previously) to the great instability of this substance.

Only in completely oxygen-free ampules protected from light is LSD absolutely stable. Such ampules, containing 100 mcg (= 0.1 mg) LSD-tartrate (tartaric acid salt of LSD) in 1 cc of aqueous solution, were produced for biological research and medicinal use by the Sandoz firm. LSD in tablets prepared with additives that inhibit oxidation, while not absolutely stable, at least keeps for a longer time. But LSD preparations often found on the black market—LSD that has been applied in solution onto sugar cubes or blotting paper—decompose in the course of weeks or a few months.

With such a highly potent substance as LSD, the correct dosage is of paramount importance. Here the tenet of Paracelsus holds good: the dose determines whether a substance acts as a remedy or as a poison. A controlled dosage, however, is not possible with preparations from the black market, whose active strength is in no way guaranteed. One of the greatest dangers of non-medicinal LSD experiments lies, therefore, in the use of such preparations of unknown provenience.

THE CASE OF DR. LEARY

Dr. Timothy Leary, who has become known worldwide in his role of drug apostle, had an extraordinarily strong influence on the diffusion of illegal LSD consumption in the United States. On the occasion of a vacation in Mexico in the year 1960, Leary had eaten the legendary "sacred mushrooms," which he had purchased from a shaman. During the mushroom inebriation he entered into a state of mystico-religious ecstasy, which he described as the deepest religious experience of his life. From then on, Dr. Leary, who at the time was a lecturer in psychology at Harvard University in Cambridge, Massachusetts, dedicated himself totally to research on the effects and possibilities of the use of psychedelic drugs. Together with his colleague Dr. Richard Alper>, he started various research projects at the university, in which LSD and psilocybin, isolated by us in the meantime, were employed.

The reintegration of convicts into society, the production of mystico-religious experiences in theologians and members of the clergy, and the furtherance of creativity in artists and writers with the help of LSD and psilocybin were tested with scientific methodology. Even persons like Aldous Huxley, Arthur Koestler, and Allen Ginsberg participated in these investigations. Particular consideration was given to the question, to what degree mental preparation and expectation of the subjects, along with the external milieu of the experiment, are able to influence the course and character of states of psychedelic inebriation.

In January 1963, Dr. Leary sent me a detailed report of these studies, in which he enthusiastically imparted the positive results obtained and gave expression to his beliefs in the advantages and very promising possibilities of such use of these active compounds. At the same time, the Sandoz firm received an inquiry about the supply of 100g LSD and 25 kg psilocybin, signed by Dr. Timothy Leary, from the Harvard University Department of Social Relations. The requirement for such an enormous quantity (the stated amounts correspond to 1 million doses of LSD and 2.5 million doses of psilocybin) was based on the planned extension of investigations to tissue, organ, and animal studies. We made the supply of these substances contingent upon the production of an import license on behalf of the U.S. health authorities. Immediately we received the order for the stated quantities of LSD and psilocybin, along with a check for $10,000 as deposit but without the required import license. Dr. Leary signed for this order, but no longer as lecturer at Harvard University, rather as president of an organization he had recently founded, the International Federation for Internal Freedom (IFIF). Because, in addition, our inquiry to the appropriate dean of Harvard University had shown that the university authorities did not approve of the continuation of the research project b

Leary and Alpert, we canceled our offer upon return of the deposit.

Shortly thereafter, Leary and Alpert were discharged from the teaching staff of Harvard University because the investigations, at first conducted in an academic milieu, had lost their scientific character. The experiments had turned into LSD parties.

The LSD trip—LSD as a ticket to an adventurous journey into new worlds of mental and physical experience—became the latest exciting fashion among academic youth, spreading rapidly from Harvard to other universities. Leary's doctrine—that LSD not only served to find the divine and to discover the self, but indeed was the most potent aphrodisiac yet discovered—surely contributed quite decisively to the rapid propagation of LSD consumption among the younger generation. Later, in an interview with the monthly magazine *Playboy*, Leary said that the intensification of sexual experience and the potentiation of sexual ecstasy by LSD was one of the chief reasons for the LSD boom.

After his expulsion from Harvard University, Leary was completely transformed from a psychology lecturer pursuing research, into the messiah of the psychedelic movement. He and his friends of the IFIF founded a psychedelic research center in lovely, scenic surroundings in Zihuatanejo, Mexico. I received a personal invitation from Dr. Leary to participate in a top-level planning session on psychedelic drugs, scheduled to take place there in August 1963. I would gladly have accepted this grand invitation, in which I was offered reimbursement for travel expenses and free lodging, in order to learn from personal observation the methods, operation, and the entire atmosphere of such a psychedelic research center, about which contradictory, to some extent very remarkable, reports were then circulating. Unfortunately, professional obligations kept me at that moment from flying to Mexico to get a picture at first hand of the controversial enterprise. The Zihuatanejo Research Center did not last long. Leary and his adherents were expelled from the country by the Mexican government. Leary, however, who had now become not only the messiah but also the martyr of the psychedelic movement, soon received help from the young New York millionaire William Hitchcock, who made a manorial house on his large estate in Millbrook, New York, available to Leary as new home and headquarters. Millbrook was also the home of another foundation for the psychedelic, transcendental way of life, the Castalia Foundation.

On a trip to India in 1965 Leary was converted to Hinduism. In the following year he founded a religious community, the League for Spiritual Discovery, whose initials give the abbreviation "LSD."

Leary's proclamation to youth, condensed in his famous slogan "Turn on, tune in, drop out!", became a central dogma of the hippie movement. Leary is one of the founding fathers of the hippie cult. The last of these three precepts, "drop out," was the challenge to escape from bourgeois life, to turn one's back on society, to give up school, studies, and employment, and to dedicate oneself wholly to the true inner universe, the study of one's own nervous system, after one has turned on with LSD. This challenge above all went beyond the psychological and religious domain to assume social and political significance. It is therefore understandable that Leary not only became the *enfant terrible* of the university and among his academic colleagues in psychology and psychiatry, but also earned the wrath of the political authorities. He was, therefore, placed under surveillance, followed, and ultimately locked in prison. The high sentences—ten years' imprisonment each for convictions in Texas and California concerning possession of LSD and marijuana, and conviction (later overturned) with a sentence of thirty years' imprisonment for marijuana smuggling—show that the punishment of these offenses was only a pretext: the real aim was to put under lock and key the seducer and instigator of youth, who could not otherwise be prosecuted. On the night of 13-14

September 1970, Leary managed to escape from the California prison in San Luis Obispo. On a detour from Algeria, where he made contact with Eldridge Cleaver, a leader of the Black Panther movement living there in exile, Leary came to Switzerland and there petitioned for political asylum.

MEETING WITH TIMOTHY LEARY

Dr. Leary lived with his wife, Rosemary, in the resort town Villars-sur-Ollon in western Switzerland. Through the intercession of Dr. Mastronardi, Dr. Leary's lawyer, contact was established between us. On 3 September 1971, I met Dr. Leary in the railway station snack bar in Lausanne. The greeting was cordial, a symbol of our fateful relationship through LSD. Leary was medium-sized, slender, resiliently active, his brown face surrounded with slightly curly hair mixed with gray, youthful, with bright, laughing eyes. This gave Leary somewhat the mark of a tennis champion rather than that of a former Harvard lecturer. We traveled by automobile to Buchillons, where in the arbor of the restaurant A la Grande Foret, over a meal of fish and a glass of white wine, the dialogue between the father and the apostle of LSD finally began.

I voiced my regret that the investigations with LSD and psilocybin at Harvard University, which had begun promisingly, had degenerated to such an extent that their continuance in an academic milieu became impossible.

My most serious remonstrance to Leary, however, concerned the propagation of LSD use among juveniles. Leary did not attempt to refute my opinions about the particular dangers of LSD for youth. He maintained, however, that I was unjustified in reproaching him for the seduction of immature persons to drug consumption, because teenagers in the United States, with regard to information and life experience, were comparable to adult Europeans. Maturity, with satiation and intellectual stagnation, would be reached very early in the United States. For that reason, he deemed the LSD experience significant, useful, and enriching, even for people still very young in years.

In this conversation, I further objected to the great publicity that Leary sought for his LSD and psilocybin investigations, since he had invited reporters from daily papers and magazines to his experiments and had mobilized radio and television. Emphasis was thereby placed on publicity rather than on objective information. Leary defended this publicity program because he felt it had been his fateful historic role to make LSD known worldwide. The overwhelmingly positive effects of such dissemination, above all among America's younger generation, would make any trifling injuries, any regrettable accidents as a result of improper use of LSD, unimportant in comparison, a small price to pay.

During this conversation, I ascertained that one did Leary an injustice by indiscriminately describing him as a drug apostle. He made a sharp distinction between psychedelic drugs—LSD, psilocybin, mescaline, hashish—of whose salutary effects he was persuaded, and the addicting narcotics morphine, heroin, etc., against whose use he repeatedly cautioned.

My impression of Dr. Leary in this personal meeting was that of a charming personage, convinced of his mission, who defended his opinions with humor yet uncompromisingly, a man who truly soared high in the clouds pervaded by beliefs in the wondrous effects of psychedelic drugs and the optimism resulting therefrom, and thus a man who tended to underrate or completely overlook practical difficulties, unpleasant facts, and dangers. Leary also showed carelessness regarding charges and dangers that concerned his own person, as his further path in life emphatically showed.

During his Swiss sojourn, I met Leary by chance once more, in February 1972, in Basel, on the occasion of a visit by Michael Horowitz, curator of the Fitz Hugh Ludlow Memorial Library in San Francisco, a library specializing in drug literature. We traveled together to my house in the country near Burg, where we resumed our conversation of the previous September. Leary appeared fidgety and detached, probably owing to a momentary indisposition, so that our discussions were less productive this time. That was my last meeting with Dr. Leary.

He left Switzerland at the end of the year, having separated from his wife, Rosemary, now accompanied by his new friend Joanna Harcourt-Smith. After a short stay in Austria, where he assisted in a documentary film about heroin, Leary and friend traveled to Afghanistan. At the airport in Kabul he was apprehended by agents of the American secret service and brought back to the San Luis Obispo prison in California.

After nothing had been heard from Leary for a long time, his name again appeared in the daily papers in summer 1975 with the announcement of a parole and early release from prison. But he was not set free until early in 1976. I learned from his friends that he was now occupied with psychological problems of space travel and with the exploration of cosmic relationships between the human nervous system and interstellar space—that is, with problems whose study would bring him no further difficulties on the part of governmental authorities.

TRAVELS IN THE UNIVERSE OF THE SOUL

Thus the Islamic scholar Dr. Rudolf Gelpke entitled his accounts of self-experiments with LSD and psilocybin, which appeared in the publication *Antaios*, for January 1962, and this title could also be used for the following descriptions of LSD experiments. LSD trips and the space flights of the astronauts are comparable in many respects. Both enterprises require very careful preparations, as far as measures for safety as well as objectives are concerned, in order to minimize dangers and to derive the most valuable results possible. The astronauts cannot remain in space nor the LSD experimenters in transcendental spheres, they have to return to earth and everyday reality, where the newly acquired experiences must be evaluated.

The following reports were selected in order to demonstrate how varied the experiences of LSD inebriation can be. The particular motivation for undertaking the experiments was also decisive in their selection. Without exception, this selection involves only reports by persons who have tried LSD not simply out of curiosity or as a sophisticated pleasure drug, but who rather experimented with it in the quest for expanded possibilities of experience of the inner and outer world; who attempted, with the help of this drug key, to unlock new "doors of perception" (William Blake); or, to continue with the comparison chosen by Rudolf Gelpke, who employed LSD to surmount the force of gravity of space and time in the accustomed worldview, in order to arrive thereby at new outlooks and understandings in the "universe of the soul."

The first two of the following research records are taken from the previously cited report by Rudolf Gelpke in *Antaios*.

DANCE OF THE SPIRITS IN THE WIND
    (0.075 mg LSD on 23 June 1961, 13:00 hours)
        After I had ingested this dose, which could be considered
        average, I conversed very animatedly with a professional
        colleague until approximately 14:00 hours. Following
        this, I proceeded alone to the Werthmuller bookstore
        where the drug now began to act most unmistakably. I
        discerned, above all, that the subjects of the books in which I
        rummaged peacefully in the back of the shop were indifferent
        to me, whereas random details of my surroundings
        suddenly stood out strongly, and somehow appeared to
        be "meaningful." ...Then, after some ten minutes, I was
        discovered by a married couple known to me, and had to let
        myself become involved in a conversation with them that, I
        admit, was by no means pleasant to me, though not really
        painful either. I listened to the conversation (even to myself)

"as from far away." The things that were discussed (the conversation dealt with Persian stories that I had translated) "belonged to another world": a world about which I could indeed express myself (I had, after all, recently still inhabited it myself and remembered the "rules of the game"!), but to which I no longer possessed any emotional connection. My interest in it was obliterated—only I did not dare to let myself observe that.

After I managed to dismiss myself, I strolled farther through the city to the marketplace. I had no "visions," saw and heard everything as usual, and yet everything was also altered in an indescribable way; "imperceptible glassy walls" everywhere. With every step that I took, I became more and more like an automaton. It especially struck me that I seemed to lose control over my facial musculature—I was convinced that my face was grown stiff, completely expressionless, empty, slack and masklike. The only reason I could still walk and put myself in motion, was because I remembered that, and how I had "earlier" gone and moved myself. But the farther back the recollection went, the more uncertain I became. I remember that my own hands somehow were in my way: I put them in my pockets, let them dangle, entwined them behind my back...as some burdensome objects, which must be dragged around with us and which no one knows quite how to stow away. I had the same reaction concerning my whole body. I no longer knew why it was there, and where I should go with it. All sense for decisions of that kind had been lost. They could only be reconstructed laboriously, taking a detour through memories from the past. It took a struggle of this kind to enable me to cover the short distance from the marketplace to my home, which I reached at about 15:10.

In no way had I had the feeling of being inebriated. What I experienced was rather a gradual mental extinction.

It was not at all frightening; but I can imagine that in
the transition to certain mental disturbances— naturally
dispersed over a greater interval—a very similar process
happens: as long as the recollection of the former individual
existence in the human world is still present, the patient who
has become unconnected can still (to some extent) find his
way about in the world: later, however, when the memories
fade and ultimately die out, he completely loses this ability.

Shortly after I had entered my room, the "glassy stupor"
gave way. I sat down, with a view out of a window, and
was at once enraptured: the window was opened wide,
the diaphanous gossamer curtains, on the other hand,
were drawn, and now a mild wind from the outside played
with these veils and with the silhouettes of potted plants
and leafy tendrils on the sill behind, which the sunlight
delineated on the curtains breathing in the breeze. This
spectacle captivated me completely. I "sank" into it, saw only
this gentle and incessant waving and rocking of the plant
shadows in the sun and the wind. I knew what "it" was, but
I sought after the name for it, after the formula, after the
"magic word" that I knew and already I had it: Totentanz,
the dance of the dead... This was what the wind and the
light were showing me on the screen of gossamer. Was it
frightening? Was I afraid? Perhaps—at first. But then a
great cheerfulness infiltrated me, and I heard the music of
silence, and even my soul danced with the redeemed shadows
to the whistle of the wind. Yes, I understood: this is the
curtain, and this curtain itself IS the secret, the "ultimate"
that it concealed. Why, therefore, tear it up? He who does
that only tears up himself. Because "there behind," behind
the curtain, is "nothing."...

Polyp from the Deep

(0.150 mg LSD on 15 April 1961, 9:15 hours)

Beginning of the effect already after about 30 minutes with strong inner agitation, trembling hands, skin chills, taste of metal on the palate.

10:00: The environment of the room transforms itself into phosphorescent waves, running hither from the feet even through my body. The skin—and above all the toes—is as electrically charged; a still constantly growing excitement hinders all clear thoughts...

10:20: I lack the words to describe my current condition. It is as if an "other" complete stranger were seizing possession of me bit by bit. Have greatest trouble writing ("inhibited" or"uninhibited"?—I don't know!).

This sinister process of an advancing self-estrangement aroused in me the feeling of powerlessness, of being helplessly delivered up. Around 10:30, through closed eyes I saw innumerable, self-intertwining threads on a red background. A sky as heavy as lead appeared to press down on everything; I felt my ego compressed in itself, and I felt like a withered dwarf... Shortly before 13:00 I escaped the more and more oppressing atmosphere of the company in the studio, in which we only hindered one another reciprocally from unfolding completely into the inebriation. I sat down in a small, empty room, on the floor, with my back to the wall, and saw through the only window on the narrow frontage opposite me a bit of gray-white cloudy sky. This, like the whole environment in general, appeared to be hopelessly normal at this moment. I was dejected, and my self seemed so repulsive and hateful to me that I had not dared (and on this day even had actually repeatedly desperately avoided) to look in a mirror or in the face of another person. I very much wished this inebriation were finally finished, but it still had my body totally in its possession. I imagined that I

*perceived, deep within its stubborn oppressive weight, how it
held my limbs surrounded with a hundred polyp arms—yes,
I actually experienced this in a mysterious rhythm; electrified
contacts, as of a real, indeed imperceptible, but sinister
omniscient being, which I addressed with a loud voice,
reviled, bid, and challenged to open combat. "It is only the
projection of evil in your self," another voice assured me. "It
is your soul monster!" This perception was like a flashing
sword. It passed through me with redeeming sharpness. The
polyp arms fell away from me—as if cut through—and
simultaneously the hitherto dull and gloomy gray-white of
the sky behind the open window suddenly scintillated like
sunlit water. As I stared at it so enchanted, it changed (for
me!) to real water: a subterranean spring overran me, which
had ruptured there all at once and now boiled up toward me,
wanted to become a storm, a lake, an ocean, with millions
and millions of drops—and on all of these drops, on every
single one of them, the light danced... As the room, window,
and sky came back into my consciousness (it was 13:25
hours), the inebriation was certainly not at an end—not
yet—but its rearguard, which passed by me during the
ensuing two hours, very much resembled the rainbow that
follows the storm.*

Both the estrangement from the environment and the
estrangement from the individual body, experienced in both
of the preceding experiments described by Gelpke—as well as
the feeling of an alien being, a demon, seizing possession of
oneself—are features of LSD inebriation that, in spite of all the
other diversity and variability of the experience, are cited in
most research reports. I have already described the possession by
the LSD demon as an uncanny experience in my first planned
self-experiment. Anxiety and terror then affected me especially
strongly, because at that time I had no way of knowing that the
demon would again release his victim.

The adventures described in the following report, by a painter, belong to a completely different type of LSD experience. This artist visited me in order to obtain my opinion about how the experience under LSD should be understood and interpreted. He feared that the profound transformation of his personal life, which had resulted from his experiment with LSD, could rest on a mere delusion. My explanation—that LSD, as a biochemical agent, only triggered his visions but had not created them and that these visions rather originated from his own soul—gave him confidence in the meaning of his transformation.

LSD EXPERIENCE OF A PAINTER

...Therefore I traveled with Eva to a solitary mountain valley. Up there in nature, I thought it would be particularly beautiful with Eva. Eva was young and attractive. Twenty years older than she, I was already in the middle of life. Despite the sorrowful consequences that I had experienced previously, as a result of erotic escapades, despite the pain and the disappointments that I inflicted on those who loved me and had believed in me, I was drawn again with irresistible power to this adventure, to Eva, to her youth. I was under the spell of this girl. Our affair indeed was only beginning, but I felt this seductive power more strongly than ever before. I knew that I could no longer resist. For the second time in my life I was again ready to desert my family, to give up my position, to break all bridges. I wanted to hurl myself uninhibitedly into this lustful inebriation with Eva. She was life, youth. Over again it cried out in me, again and again to drain the cup of lust and life until the last drop, until death and perdition. Let the Devil fetch me later on! I had indeed long ago done away with God and the Devil. They were for me only human inventions, which came to be utilized by a skeptical, unscrupulous minority, in order to suppress and exploit a believing, naive majority. I wanted

to have nothing to do with this mendacious social moral. To enjoy, at all costs, I wished to enjoy *et apres nous te deluge.* "What is wife to me, what is child to me—let them go begging, if they are hungry." I also perceived the institution of marriage as a social lie. The marriage of my parents and marriages of my acquaintances seemed to confirm that sufficiently for me. Couples remained together because it was more convenient; they were accustomed to it, and "yes, if it weren't for the children…" Under the pretense of a good marriage, each tormented the other emotionally, to the point of rashes and stomach ulcers, or each went his own way. Everything in me rebelled against the thought of having to love only one and the same woman a life long. I frankly perceived that as repugnant and unnatural. Thus stood my inner disposition on that portentous summer evening at the mountain lake.

At seven o'clock in the evening both of us took a moderately strong dose of LSD, some 0.1 milligrams. Then we strolled along about the lake and then sat on the bank. We threw stones in the water and watched the forming wave circles. We felt a slight inner restlessness. Around eight o'clock we entered the hotel lounge and ordered tea and sandwiches. Some guests still sat there, telling jokes and laughing loudly. They winked at us. Their eyes sparkled strangely. We felt strange and distant and had the feeling that they would notice something in us. Outside it slowly became dark. We decided only reluctantly to go to our hotel room. A street without lights led along the black lake to the distant guest house. As I switched on the light, the granite staircase, leading from the shore road to the house, appeared to flame up from step to step. Eva quivered all at once, frightened. "Hellish" went through my mind, and all of a sudden horror passed through my limbs, and I knew: now it's going to turn out badly. From afar, from the village, a *clock struck nine.*

Scarcely were we in our room, when Eva threw herself on the bed and looked at me with wide eyes. It was not in the least possible to think of love. I sat down on the edge of the bed and held both of Eva's hands. Then came the terror. We sank into a deep, indescribable horror, which neither of us understood.

"Look in my eyes, look at me," I implored Eva, yet again and again her gaze was averted from me, and then she cried out loud in terror and trembled all over her body. There was no way out. Outside was only gloomy night and the deep, black lake. In the public house all the lights were extinguished; the people had probably gone to sleep. What would they have said if they could see us now? Possibly they would summon the police, and then everything would become still much worse. A drug scandal – intolerable agonizing thoughts.

We could no longer move from the spot. We sat there surrounded by four wooden walls whose board joints shone infernally. It became more unbearable all the time. Suddenly the door was opened and "something dreadful" entered. Eva cried out wildly and hid herself under the bed covers. Once again a cry. The horror under the covers was yet worse. "Look straight in my eyes!" I called to her, but she rolled her eyes back and forth as though out of her mind. She is becoming insane, I realized. In desperation I seized her by the hair so that she could no longer turn her face away from me. I saw dreadful fear in her eyes. Everything around us was hostile and threatening, as if everything wanted to attack us in the next moment. You must protect Eva, you must bring her through until morning, then the effects will discontinue, I said to myself. Then again, however, I plunged into nameless horror. There was no more time or reason; it seemed as if this condition would never end.

The objects in the room were animated to caricatures;
everything on all sides sneered scornfully. I saw Eva's
yellow-black striped shoes, which I had found so stimulating,
appearing as two large, evil wasps crawling on the floor. The
water piping above the washbasin changed to a dragon head,
whose eyes, the two water taps, observed me malevolently.
My first name, George, came into my mind, and all at once I
felt like Knight George, who must fight for Eva.

Eva's cries tore me from these thoughts. Bathed in
perspiration and trembling, she fastened herself to me. "I am
thirsty," she moaned. With great effort, without releasing
Eva's hand, I succeeded in getting a glass of water for her.
But the water seemed slimy and viscous, was poisonous, and
we could not quench our thirst with it. The two night-table
lamps glowed with a strange brightness, in an infernal light.
The clock struck twelve.

This is hell, I thought. There is indeed no Devil
and no demons, and yet they were perceptible in us,
filled up the room, and tormented us with unimaginable
terror. Imagination, or not? Hallucinations, projections?
Insignificant questions when confronted with the reality
of fear that was fixed in our bodies and shook us: the fear
alone, it existed. Some passages from Huxley's book THE
DOORS OF PERCEPTION came to me and brought me brief
comfort. I looked at Eva, at this whimpering, horrified
being in her torment, and felt great remorse and pity. She
had become strange to me; I scarcely recognized her any
longer. She wore a fine golden chain around her neck with
the medallion of the Virgin Mary. It was a gift from her
younger brother. I noticed how a benevolent, comforting
radiation, which was connected with pure love, emanated
from this necklace. But then the terror broke loose again,
as if to our final destruction. I needed my whole strength to
constrain Eva. Loudly I heard the electrical meter ticking

*weirdly outside of the door, as if it wanted to make a most
important, evil, devastating announcement to me in the
next moment. Disdain, derision, and malignity again
whispered out of all nooks and crevices. There, in the midst
of this agony, I perceived the ringing of cowbells from afar
as a wonderful, promising music. Yet soon it became silent
again, and renewed fear and dread once again set in. As a
drowning man hopes for a rescuing plank, so I wished that
the cows would yet again want to draw near the house.
But everything remained quiet, and only the threatening
tick and hum of the current meter buzzed round us like an
invisible, malevolent insect.*

*Morning finally dawned. With great relief I noticed
how the chinks in the window shutters lit up. Now I could
leave Eva to herself; she had quieted down. Exhausted,
she closed her eyes and fell asleep. Shocked and deeply sad,
I still sat on the edge of the bed. Gone was my pride and
self-assurance; all that remained of me was a small heap
of misery. I examined myself in the mirror and started:
I had become ten years older in the course of the night.
Downcast, I stared at the light of the night table lamp
with the hideous shade of intertwined plastic cords. All
at once the light seemed to become brighter, and in the
plastic cords it began to sparkle and to twinkle; it glowed
like diamonds and gems of all colors, and an overwhelming
feeling of happiness welled up in me. All at once, lamp, room,
and Eva disappeared, and I found myself in a wonderful,
fantastic landscape. It was comparable to the interior of an
immense Gothic church nave, with infinitely many columns
and Gothic arches. These consisted, however, not of stone,
but rather of crystal. Bluish, yellowish, milky, and clearly
transparent crystal columns surrounded me like trees in an
open forest. Their points and arches became lost in dizzying
heights. A bright light appeared before my inner eye, and a*

wonderful, gentle voice spoke to me out of the light. I did not hear it with my external ear, but rather perceived it, as if it were clear thoughts that arise in one.

I realized that in the horror of the passing night I had experienced my own individual condition: selfishness. My egotism had kept me separated from mankind and had led me to inner isolation. I had loved only myself, not my neighbor; loved only the gratification that the other offered me. The world had existed only for the satisfaction of my greed. I had become tough, cold, and cynical. Hell, therefore, had signified that: egotism and lovelessness. Therefore everything had seemed strange and unconnected to me, so scornful and threatening. Amid flowing tears, I was enlightened with the knowledge that true love means surrender of selfishness and that it is not desires but rather selfless love that forms the bridge to the heart of our fellow man. Waves of ineffable happiness flowed through my body. I had experienced the grace of God. But how could it be possible that it was radiating toward me, particularly out of this cheap lampshade? Then the inner voice answered: God is in everything.

The experience at the mountain lake has given me the certainty that beyond the ephemeral, material world there also exists an imperishable, spiritual reality, which is our true home. I am now on my way home.

For Eva everything remained just a bad dream. We broke up a short time thereafter.

The following notes kept by a twenty-five-year-old advertising agent are contained in *The LSD Story* by John Cashman (Fawcett Publications, Greenwich, CT, 1966). They were included in this selection of LSD reports, along with the preceding example, because the progression that they describe—from terrifying visions to extreme euphoria, a kind of death-rebirth cycle—is characteristic of many LSD experiments.

A JOYOUS SONG OF BEING

*My first experience with LSD came at the home of a
close friend who served as my guide. The surroundings were
comfortably familiar and relaxing. I took two ampules (200
micrograms) of LSD mixed in half a glass of distilled water.
The experience lasted for close to eleven hours, from eight
o'clock on a Saturday evening until very nearly seven o'clock
the next morning. I have no firm point of comparison, but I
am positive that no saint ever saw more glorious or joyously
beautiful visions or experienced a more blissful state of
transcendence. My powers to convey the miracles are shabby
and far too inadequate to the task at hand. A sketch, and
an artless one at that, must suffice where only the hand of a
great master working from a complete palette could do justice
to the subject. I must apologize for my own limitations in
this feeble attempt to reduce the most remarkable experience
of my life to mere words. My superior smile at the fumbling,
halting attempts of others in their attempts to explain the
heavenly visions to me has been transformed into a knowing
smile of a conspirator—the common experience requires no
words.*

*My first thought after drinking the LSD was that it
was having absolutely no effect. They had told me thirty
minutes would produce the first sensation, a tingling of
the skin. There was no tingling. I commented on this and
was told to relax and wait. For the lack of anything else
to do I stared at the dial light of the table radio, nodding
my head to a jazz piece I did not recognize. I think it
was several minutes before I realized that the light was
changing color kaleidoscopically with the different pitch
of the musical sounds, bright reds and yellows in the high
register, deep purple in the low. I laughed. I had no idea
when it had started. I simply knew it had. I closed my eyes,
but the colored notes were still there. I was overcome by*

the remarkable brilliance of the colors. I tried to talk, to explain what I was seeing, the vibrant and luminous colors. Somehow it didn't seem important. With my eyes open, the radiant colors flooded the room, folding over on top of one another in rhythm with the music. Suddenly I was aware that the colors were the music. The discovery did not seem startling. Values, so cherished and guarded, were becoming unimportant. I wanted to talk about the colored music, but I couldn't. I was reduced to uttering one-syllable words while polysyllabic impressions tumbled through my mind with the speed of light.

The dimensions of the room were changing, now sliding into a fluttering diamond shape, then straining into an oval shape as if someone were pumping air into the room, expanding it to the bursting point. I was having trouble focusing on objects. They would melt into fuzzy masses of nothing or sail off into space, self-propelled, slow-motion trips that were of acute interest to me. I tried to check the time on my watch, but I was unable to focus on the hands. I thought of asking for the time, but the thought passed. I was too busy seeing and listening. The sounds were exhilarating, the sights remarkable. I was completely entranced. I have no idea how long this lasted. I do know the egg came next.

The egg, large, pulsating, and a luminous green, was there before I actually saw it. I sensed it was there. It hung suspended about halfway between where I sat and the far wall. I was intrigued by the beauty of the egg. At the same time I was afraid it would drop to the floor and break. I didn't want the egg to break. It seemed most important that the egg should not break. But even as I thought of this, the egg slowly dissolved and revealed a great multihued flower that was like no flower I have ever seen. Its incredibly exquisite petals opened on the room, spraying indescribable colors in every direction. I felt the colors and heard them as they played across my body, cool and warm, reedlike and tinkling.

The first tinge of apprehension came later when I saw the center of the flower slowly eating away at the petals, a black, shiny center that appeared to be formed by the backs of a thousand ants. It ate away the petals at an agonizingly slow pace. I wanted to scream for it to stop or to hurry up. I was pained by the gradual disappearance of the beautiful petals as if being swallowed by an insidious disease. Then in a flash of insight I realized to my horror that the black thing was actually devouring me. I was the flower and this foreign, creeping thing was eating me!

I shouted or screamed, I really don't remember. I was too full of fear and loathing. I heard my guide say: "Easy now. Just go with it. Don't fight it. Go with it." I tried, but the hideous blackness caused such repulsion that I screamed: "I can't! For God's sake help me! Help me!" The voice was soothing, reassuring: "Let it come. Everything is all right. Don't worry. Go with it. Don't fight."

I felt myself dissolving into the terrifying apparition, my body melting in waves into the core of blackness, my mind stripped of ego and life and, yes even death. In one great crystal instant I realized that I was immortal. I asked the question: "Am I dead?" But the question had no meaning. Meaning was meaningless. Suddenly there was white light and the shimmering beauty of unity. There was light everywhere, white light with a clarity beyond description. I was dead and I was born and the exultation was pure and holy. My lungs were bursting with the joyful song of being. There was unity and life and the exquisite love that filled my being was unbounded. My awareness was acute and complete. I saw God and the devil and all the saints and I knew the truth. I felt myself flowing into the cosmos, levitated beyond all restraint, liberated to swim in the blissful radiance of the heavenly visions.

I wanted to shout and sing of miraculous new life and sense and form, of the joyous beauty and the whole mad ecstasy of loveliness. I knew and understood all there is to know and understand. I was immortal, wise beyond wisdom, and capable of love, of all loves. Every atom of my body and soul had seen and felt God. The world was warmth and goodness. There was no time, no place, no me. There was only cosmic harmony. It was all there in the white light. With every fiber of my being I knew it was so.

I embraced the enlightenment with complete abandonment. As the experience receded I longed to hold onto it and tenaciously fought against the encroachment of the realities of time and place. For me, the realities of our limited existence were no longer valid. I had seen the ultimate realities and there would be no others. As I was slowly transported back to the tyranny of clocks and schedules and petty hatreds, I tried to talk of my trip, my enlightenment, the horrors, the beauty, all of it. I must have been babbling like an idiot. My thoughts swirled at a fantastic rate, but the words couldn't keep pace. My guide smiled and told me he understood.

The preceding collection of reports on "travels in the universe of the soul," even though they encompass such dissimilar experiences, are still not able to establish a complete picture of the broad spectrum of all possible reactions to LSD, which extends from the most sublime spiritual, religious, and mystical experiences, down to gross psychosomatic disturbances. Cases of LSD sessions have been described in which the stimulation of fantasy and of visionary experience, as expressed in the LSD reports assembled here, is completely absent, and the experimenter was for the whole time in a state of ghastly physical and mental discomfort, or even felt severely ill.

Reports about the modification of sexual experience under

the influence of LSD are also contradictory. Since stimulation of all sensory perception is an essential feature of LSD effects, the sensual orgy of sexual intercourse can undergo unimaginable enhancements. Cases have also been described, however, in which LSD led not to the anticipated erotic paradise, but rather to a purgatory or even to the hell of frightful extinction of every perception and to a lifeless vacuum.

Such a variety and contradiction of reactions to a drug is found only in LSD and the related hallucinogens. The explanation for this lies in the complexity and variability of the conscious and subconscious minds of people, which LSD is able to penetrate and to bring to life as experienced reality.

Chapter VI

The Mexican Relatives of LSD

THE SACRED MUSHROOM TEONANACATL.

LATE IN 1956 a notice in the daily paper caught my interest. Among some Indians in southern Mexico, American researchers had discovered mushrooms that were eaten in religious ceremonies and that produced an inebriated condition accompanied by hallucinations.

Since, outside of the mescaline cactus found also in Mexico, no other drug was known at the time that, like LSD, produced hallucinations, I would have liked to establish contact with these researchers, in order to learn details about these hallucinogenic mushrooms. But there were no names and addresses in the short newspaper article, so that it was impossible to get further information. Nevertheless, the mysterious mushrooms, whose chemical investigation would be a tempting problem, stayed in my thoughts from then on.

As it later turned out, LSD was the reason that these mushrooms found their way into my laboratory, without my assistance, at the beginning of the following year.

Through the mediation of Dr. Yves Dunant, at the time director of the Paris branch of Sandoz, an inquiry came to the pharmaceutical research management in Basel from Professor Roger Heim, director of the Laboratoire de Cryptogamie of the Museum National d'Histoire Naturelle in Paris, asking whether we were interested in carrying out the chemical investigation of the Mexican hallucinogenic mushrooms. With great joy I declared myself ready to begin this work in my department, in the laboratories for natural product research. That was to be my link to the exciting investigations of the Mexican sacred mushrooms, which were already broadly advanced in the ethnomycological and botanical aspects.

For a long time the existence of these magic mushrooms had remained an enigma. The history of their rediscovery is presented at first hand in the magnificent two-volume standard work of ethnomycology, *Mushrooms, Russia and History* (Pantheon Books, New York, 1957), for the authors, the American researchers Valentina Pavlovna Wasson and her husband, R. Gordon Wasson, played a decisive role in this rediscovery. The following descriptions of the fascinating history of these mushrooms are taken from the Wassons' book.

The first written evidence of the use of inebriating mushrooms on festival occasions, or in the course of religious ceremonies and magically oriented healing practices, is found among the Spanish chroniclers and naturalists of the sixteenth century, who entered the country soon after the conquest of Mexico by Hernan Cortes. The most important of these witnesses is the Franciscan friar Bernardino de Sahagun, who mentions the magic mushrooms and describes their effects and their use in several passages of his famous historical work, Historia General de tas Cosas de Nueva Espana, written between the years 1529 and 1590. Thus he describes, for example, how merchants celebrated the return home from a successful business trip with a mushroom party:

> *Coming at the very first, at the time of feasting, they ate mushrooms when, as they said, it was the hour of the blowing of the flutes. Not yet did they partake of food; they drank only chocolate during the night. And they ate mushrooms with honey. When already the mushrooms were taking effect, there was dancing, there was weeping... Some saw in a vision that they would die in war. Some saw in a vision that they would be devoured by wild beasts... Some saw in a vision that they would become rich, wealthy. Some saw in a vision that they would buy slaves, would become*

slave owners. Some saw in a vision that they would commit adultery [and so] would have their heads bashed in, would be stoned to death... Some saw in a vision that they would perish in the water. Some saw in a vision that they would pass to tranquility in death. Some saw in a vision that they would fall from the housetop, tumble to their death... . All such things they saw... And when [the effects of] the mushroom ceased, they conversed with one another, spoke of what they had seen in the vision.

In a publication from the same period, Diego Duran, a Dominican friar, reported that inebriating mushrooms were eaten at the great festivity on the occasion of the accession to the throne of Moctezuma II, the famed emperor of the Aztecs, in the year 1502. A passage in the seventeenth-century chronicle of Don Jacinto de la Serna refers to the use of these mushrooms in a religious framework:

And what happened was that there had come to [the village] an Indian... and his name was Juan Chichiton... and he had brought the red-colored mushrooms that are gathered in the uplands, and with them he had committed a great idolatry... In the house where everyone had gathered on the occasion of a saint's feast... the teponastli [an Aztec percussion instrument] was playing and singing was going on the whole night through. After most of the night had passed, Juan Chichiton, who was the priest for that solumn rite, to all of those present at the fiesta gave the mushrooms to eat, after the manner of Communion, and gave them pulque to drink... so that they all went out of their heads, a shame it was to see.

In Nahuatl, the language of the Aztecs, these mushrooms were described as *teonanactl*, which can be translated as "sacred mushroom."

There are indications that ceremonial use of such mushrooms reaches far back into pre-Columbian times. So-called mushroom stones have been found in El Salvador, Guatemala, and the contiguous mountainous districts of Mexico. These are stone sculptures in the form of pileate mushroom, on whose stem the face or the form of a god or an animal-like demon is carved. Most are about 30 cm high. The oldest examples, according to archaeologists, date back to before 500 B.C.

R. G. Wasson argues, quite convincingly, that there is a connection between these mushroom stones and teonanacatl. If true, this means that the mushroom cult, the magico-medicinal and religious-ceremonial use of the magic mushrooms, is more than two thousand years old.

To the Christian missionaries, the inebriating, vision- and hallucination-producing effects of these mushrooms seemed to be Devil's work. They therefore tried, with all the means in their power, to extirpate their use. But they succeeded only partially, for the Indians have continued secretly down to our time to utilize the mushroom teonanacatl, which was sacred to them.

Strange to say, the reports in the old chronicles about the use of magic mushrooms remained unnoticed during the following centuries, probably because they were considered products of the imagination of a superstitious age.

All traces of the existence of "sacred mushrooms" were in danger of becoming obliterated once and for all, when, in 1915, an American botanist of repute, Dr. W. E. Safford, in an address before the Botanical Society in Washington and in a scientific publication, advanced the thesis that no such thing as magic mushrooms had ever existed at all: the Spanish chroniclers had taken the mescaline cactus for a mushroom! Even if false, this proposition of Safford's served nevertheless to direct the attention of the scientific world to the riddle of the mysterious mushrooms.

It was the Mexican physician Dr. Blas Pablo Reko who first openly disagreed with Safford's interpretation and who found evidence that mushrooms were still employed in medicinal-religious ceremonies even in our time, in remote districts of the southern mountains of Mexico. But not until the years 1938 did the anthropologist Robert J. Weitlaner and Dr. Richard Evans Schultes, a botanist from Harvard University, find actual mushrooms in that region, which were used there for this ceremonial purpose; and only in 1938 could a group of young American anthropologists, under the direction of Jean Bassett Johnson, attend a secret nocturnal mushroom ceremony for the first time. This was in Huautla de Jimenez, the capital of the Mazatec country, in the State of Oaxaca. But these researchers were only spectators, they were not permitted to partake of the mushrooms. Johnson reported on the experience in a Swedish journal (*Ethnological Studies* 9, 1939).

Then exploration of the magic mushrooms was interrupted. World War II broke out. Schultes, at the behest of the American government, had to occupy himself with rubber production in the Amazon territory, and Johnson was killed after the Allied landing in North Africa.

It was the American researchers, the married couple Dr. Valentina Pavlovna Wasson and her husband, R. Gordon Wasson, who again took up the problem from the ethnographic aspect. R. G. Wasson was a banker, vice-president of the J. P. Morgan Co. in New York. His wife, who died in 1958, was a pediatrician. The Wassons began their work in 1953, in the Mazatec village Huautla de Jimenez, where fifteen years earlier J. B. Johnson and others had established the continued existence of the ancient Indian mushroom cult. They received especially valuable information from an American missionary who had been active there for many years, Eunice V. Pike, member of the Wycliffe Bible Translators. Thanks to her knowledge of the native language and her ministerial association with the inhabitants, Pike had information about the significance of the magic mushrooms that nobody else possessed. During several lengthy sojourns in Huautla and environs, the Wassons were able to study the present use of the mushrooms in detail and compare it with the

descriptions in the old chronicles. This showed that the belief
in the "sacred mushrooms" was still prevalent in that region.
However, the Indians kept their beliefs a secret from strangers.
It took great tact and skill, therefore, to gain the confidence of
the indigenous population and to receive insight into this secret
domain.

In the modern form of the mushroom cult, the old religious
ideas and customs are mingled with Christian ideas and Christian
terminology. Thus the mushrooms are often spoken of as the
blood of Christ, because they will grow only where a drop of
Christ's blood has fallen on the earth. According to another
notion, the mushrooms sprout where a drop of saliva from
Christ's mouth has moistened the ground, and it is therefore Jesus
Christ himself who speaks through the mushrooms.

The mushroom ceremony follows the form of a consultation.
The seeker of advice or a sick person or his or her family
questions a "wise man" or a "wise woman," *asabio orsabia*, also
named *curandero* or *curandera*, in return for a modest payment.
Curandero can best be translated into English as "healing priest,"
for his function is that of a physician as well as that of a priest,
both being found only rarely in these remote regions. In the
Mazatec language the healing priest is called *co-ta-ci-ne*, which
means "one who knows." He eats the mushroom in the framework
of a ceremony that always takes place at night. The other persons
present at the ceremony may sometimes receive mushrooms as
well, yet a much greater dose always goes to the curandero. The
performance is executed with the accompaniment of prayers
and entreaties, while the mushrooms are incensed briefly over
a basin, in which copal (an incense-like resin) is burned. In
complete darkness, at times by candlelight, while the others
present lie quietly on their straw mats, the curandero, kneeling
or sitting, prays and sings before a type of altar bearing a crucifix,
an image of a saint, or some other object of worship. Under the
influence of the sacred mushrooms, the curandero counsels in

a visionary state, in which even the inactive observers more or less participate. In the monotonous song of the curandero, the mushroom teonanacatl gives its answers to the questions posed. It says whether the diseased person will live or die, which herbs will effect the cure; it reveals who has killed a specific person, or who has stolen the horse; or it makes known how a distant relative fares, and so forth.

The mushroom ceremony not only has the function of a consulation of the type described; for the Indians it also has a meaning in many respects similar to the Holy Communion for the believing Christian. From many utterances of the natives it could be inferred that they believe that God has given the Indians the sacred mushroom because they are poor and possess no doctors and medicines; and also, because they cannot read, in particular the Bible, God can therefore speak directly to them through the mushroom. The missionary Eunice V. Pike even alluded to the difficulties that result from explaining the Christian message, the written word, to a people who believe they possess a means—the sacred mushrooms of course—to make God's will known to them in a direct, clear manner: yes, the mushrooms permit them to see into heaven and to establish communication with God himself.

The Indians' reverence for the sacred mushrooms is also evident in their belief that they can be eaten only by a "clean" person. "Clean" here means ceremonially clean, and that term among other things includes sexual abstinence at least four days before and after ingestion of the mushrooms. Certain rules must also be observed in gathering the mushrooms. With nonobservance of these commandments, the mushrooms can make the person who eats them insane, or can even kill.

The Wassons had undertaken their first expedition to the Mazatec country in 1953, but not until 1955 did they succeed in overcoming the shyness and reserve of the Mazatec friends they had managed to make, to the point of being admitted as active participants in a mushroom ceremony. R. Gordon Wasson and his companion, the photographer Allan Richardson, were given sacred mushrooms to eat at the end of June 1955, on the occasion of a nocturnal mushroom ceremony. They thereby became in all likelihood the first outsiders, the first whites, ever permitted to take teonanacatl.

In the second volume of *Mushrooms, Russia and History*, in enraptured words, Wasson describes how the mushroom seized possession of him completely, although he had tried to struggle against its effects, in order to be able to remain an objective observer. First he saw geometric, colored patterns, which then took on architectural characteristics. Next followed visions of splendid colonnades, palaces of supernatural harmony and magnificence embellished with precious gems, triumphal cars drawn by fabulous creatures as they are known only from mythology, and landscapes of fabulous luster. Detached from the body, the spirit soared timelessly in a realm of fantasy among images of a higher reality and deeper meaning than those of the ordinary, everyday world. The essence of life, the ineffable, seemed to be on the verge of being unlocked, but the ultimate door failed to open.

This experience was the final proof, for Wasson, that the magical powers attributed to the mushrooms actually existed and were not merely superstition.

In order to introduce the mushrooms to scientific research, Wasson had earlier established an association with mycologist Professor Roger Heim of Paris. Accompanying the Wassons on further expeditions into the Mazatec country, Heim conducted the botanical identification of the sacred mushrooms. He showed that they were gilled mushrooms from the family *Strophariaceae*, about a dozen different species not previously described scientifically, the greatest part belonging to the genus *Psilocybe*. Professor Heim also succeeded in cultivating some of the species in the laboratory. The mushroom *Psilocybe mexicana* turned out to be especially suitable for artificial cultivation.

Chemical investigations ran parallel with these botanical studies on the magic mushrooms, with the goal of extracting the hallucinogenically active principle from the mushroom material and preparing it in chemically pure form. Such investigations were carried out at Professor Heim's instigation in the chemical laboratory of the Museum National d'Histoire Naturelle in Paris, and work teams were occupied with this problem in the United States in the research laboratories of two large pharmaceutical companies: Merck, and Smith, Kline and French. The American laboratories had obtained some of the mushrooms from R. G. Wasson and had gathered others themselves in the Sierra Mazateca.

As the chemical investigations in Paris and in the United States turned out to be ineffectual, Professor Heim addressed this matter to our firm, as mentioned at the beginning of this chapter, because he felt that our experimental experience with LSD, related to the magic mushrooms by similar activity, could be of use in the isolation attempts. Thus it was LSD that showed teonanacatl the way into our laboratory.

As director of the department of natural products of the Sandoz pharmaceutical-chemical research laboratories at that time, I wanted to assign the investigation of the magic mushrooms to one of my coworkers. However, nobody showed much eagerness to take on this problem because it was known that LSD and everything connected with it were scarcely popular subjects with the top management. Because the enthusiasm necessary for successful endeavors cannot be commanded, and because the enthusiasm was already present in me as far as this problem was concerned, I decided to conduct the investigation myself.

Some 100 g of dried mushrooms of the species *Psilocybe mexicana*, cultivated by Professor Heim in the laboratory, were available for the beginning of the chemical analysis. My laboratory assistant, Hans Tscherter, who during our decade-long collaboration, had developed into a very capable helper, completely familiar with my manner of work, aided me in the extraction and isolation attempts. Since there were no clues at all concerning the chemical properties of the active principle we sought, the isolation attempts had to be conducted on the basis of the effects of the extract fractions. But none of the various extracts showed an unequivocal effect, either in the mouse or the dog, which could have pointed to the presence of hallucinogenic principles. It therefore became doubtful whether the mushrooms cultivated and dried in Paris were still active at all. That could only be determined by experimenting with this mushroom material on a human being. As in the case of LSD, I made this fundamental experiment myself, since it is not appropriate for researchers to ask anyone else to perform self-experiments that they require for their own investigations, especially if they entail, as in this case, a certain risk.

In this experiment I ate 32 dried specimens of *Psilocybe mexicana*, which together weighed 2.4 g. This amount corresponded to an average dose, according to the reports of Wasson and Heim, as it is used by the curanderos. The mushrooms displayed a strong psychic effect, as the following extract from the report on that experiment shows:

Thirty minutes after my taking the mushrooms, the exterior world began to undergo a strange transformation. Everything assumed a Mexican character. As I was perfectly well aware that my knowledge of the Mexican origin of the mushroom would lead me to imagine only Mexican scenery, I tried deliberately to look on my environment as I knew it normally. But all voluntary efforts to look at things in their customary forms and colors proved ineffective. Whether my eyes were closed or open, I saw only Mexican motifs and colors. When the doctor supervising the experiment bent over me to check my blood pressure, he was transformed into an Aztec priest and I would not have been astonished if he had drawn an obsidian knife. In spite of the seriousness of

*the situation, it amused me to see how the Germanic face
of my colleague had acquired a purely Indian expression.
At the peak of the intoxication, about 1 1/2 hours after
ingestion of the mushrooms, the rush of interior pictures,
mostly abstract motifs rapidly changing in shape and color,
reached such an alarming degree that I feared that I would
be torn into this whirlpool of form and color and would
dissolve. After about six hours the dream came to an end.
Subjectively, I had no idea how long this condition had
lasted. I felt my return to everyday reality to be a happy
return from a strange, fantastic but quite real world to an
old and familiar home.*

This self-experiment showed once again that human beings
react much more sensitively than animals to psychoactive
substances. We had already reached the same conclusion in
experimenting with LSD on animals, as described in an earlier
chapter of this book. It was not inactivity of the mushroom
material, but rather the deficient reaction capability of the
research animals vis-a-vis such a type of active principle, that
explained why our extracts had appeared inactive in the mouse
and dog.

Because the assay on human subjects was the only test at
our disposal for the detection of the active extract fractions, we
had no other choice than to perform the testing on ourselves
if we wanted to carry on the work and bring it to a successful
conclusion. In the self-experiment just described, a strong reaction
lasting several hours was produced by 2.4 g dried mushrooms.
Therefore, in the sequel we used samples corresponding to only
one-third of this amount, namely 0.8 g dried mushrooms. If these
samples contained the active principle, they would only provoke
a mild effect that impaired the ability to work for a short time,
but this effect would still be so distinct that the inactive fractions
and those containing the active principle could unequivocally be
differentiated from one another. Several coworkers and colleagues

volunteered as guinea pigs for this series of tests.

PSILOCYBIN AND PSILOCIN

With the help of this reliable test on human subjects, the active principle could be isolated, concentrated, and transformed into a chemically pure state by means of the newest separation methods. Two new substances, which I named psilocybin and psilocin, were thereby obtained in the form of colorless crystals.

These results were published in March 1958 in the journal *Experientia*, in collaboration with Professor Heim and with my colleagues Dr. A. Brack and Dr. H. Kobel, who had provided greater quantities of mushroom material for these investigations after they had essentially improved the laboratory cultivation of the mushrooms.

Some of my coworkers at the time—Drs. A. J. Frey, H. Ott, T. Petrzilka, and F. Troxler—then participated in the next steps of these investigations, the determination of the chemical structure of psilocybin and psilocin and the subsequent synthesis of these compounds, the results of which were published in the November 1958 issue of Experientia. The chemical structures of these mushroom factors deserve special attention in several respects. Psilocybin and psilocin belong, like LSD, to the indole compounds, the biologically important class of substances found in the plant and animal kingdoms. Particular chemical features common to both the mushroom substances and LSD show that psilocybin and psilocin are closely related to LSD, not only with regard to psychic effects but also to their chemical structures. Psilocybin is the phosphoric acid ester of psilocin and, as such, is the first and hitherto only phosphoric-acid-containing indole compound discovered in nature. The phosphoric acid residue does not contribute to the activity, for the phosphoric-acid-free psilocin is just as active as psilocybin, but it makes the molecule more stable. While psilocin is readily decomposed by the oxygen in air, psilocybin is a stable substance.

Psilocybin and psilocin possess a chemical structure very similar to the brain factor serotonin. As was already mentioned in the chapter on animal experiments and biological research, serotonin plays an important role in the chemistry of brain functions. The two mushroom factors, like LSD, block the effects of serotonin in pharmacological experiments on different organs. Other pharmacological properties of psilocybin and psilocin are also similar to those of LSD. The main difference consists in the quantitative activity, in animal as well as human experimentation. The average active dose of psilocybin or psilocin in human beings amounts to 10 mg (0.01 g); accordingly, these two substances are more than 100 times less active than LSD, of which 0.1 mg constitutes a strong dose. Moreover, the effects of the mushroom factors last only four to six hours, much shorter than the effects of LSD (eight to twelve hours).

The total synthesis of psilocybin and psilocin, without the aid of the mushrooms, could be developed into a technical process, which would allow these substances to be produced on a large scale. Synthetic production is more rational and cheaper than extraction from the mushrooms.

Thus with the isolation and synthesis of the active principles, the demystification of the magic mushrooms was accomplished. The compounds whose wondrous effects led the Indians to believe for millennia that a god was residing in the mushrooms had their chemical structures elucidated and could be produced synthetically in flasks.

Just what progress in scientific knowledge was accomplished by natural products research in this case? Essentially, when all is said and done, we can only say that the mystery of the wondrous effects of teonanacatl was reduced to the mystery of the effects of two crystalline substances—since these effects cannot be explained by science either, but can only be described.

A Voyage into the Universe of the Soul with Psilocybin

The relationship between the psychic effects of psilocybin and those of LSD, their visionary hallucinatory character, is evident in the following report from *Antaios*, of a psilocybin experiment by Dr. Rudolf Gelpke. He has characterized his experiences with LSD and psilocybin, as already mentioned in a previous chapter, as "travels in the universe of the soul."

Where Time Stands Still

> *(10 mg psilocybin, 6 April 1961, 10:20)*
>
> *After ca. 20 minutes, beginning effects: serenity, speechlessness, mild but pleasant dizzy sensation, and "pleasureful deep breathing."*
>
> *10:50 Strong! dizziness, can no longer concentrate .*
>
> *10:55 Excited, intensity of colors: everything pink to red.*
>
> *11:05 The world concentrates itself there on the center of the table. Colors very intense.*
>
> *11:10 A divided being, unprecedented—how can I describe this sensation of life? Waves, different selves, must control me.*
>
> *Immediately after this note I went outdoors, leaving the breakfast table, where I had eaten with Dr. H. and our wives, and lay down on the lawn. The inebriation pushed rapidly to its climax. Although I had firmly resolved to make constant notes, it now seemed to me a complete waste of time, the motion of writing infinitely slow, the possibilities of verbal expression unspeakably paltry—measured by the flood of inner experience that inundated me and threatened to burst me. It seemed to me that 100 years would not be sufficient to describe the fullness of experience of a single minute. At the beginning, optical impressions predominated: I saw with delight the boundless succession of rows of trees in the nearby forest. Then the tattered clouds in the sunny sky rapidly piled up with silent and breathtaking majesty to a superimposition of thousands of layers—heaven on*

heaven—and I waited then expecting that up there in the
next moment something completely powerful, unheard of,
not yet existing, would appear or happen—would I behold
a god? But only the expectation remained, the presentiment,
this hovering, "on the threshold of the ultimate feeling."
... Then I moved farther away (the proximity of others
disturbed me) and lay down in a nook of the garden on a
sun-warmed wood pile—my fingers stroked this wood with
overflowing, animal-like sensual affection. At the same time
I was submerged within myself; it was an absolute climax:
a sensation of bliss pervaded me, a contented happiness—I
found myself behind my closed eyes in a cavity full of brick-red
ornaments, and at the same time in the "center of the universe
of consummate calm." I knew everything was good—the
cause and origins of everything was good. But at the same
moment I also understood the suffering and the loathing, the
depression and misunderstanding of ordinary life: there one
is never "total," but instead divided, cut in pieces, and split
up into the tiny fragments of seconds, minutes, hours, days,
weeks, and years; there one is a slave of Moloch time, which
devoured one piecemeal; one is condemned to stammering,
bungling, and patchwork; one must drag about with oneself
the perfection and absolute, the togetherness of all things;
the eternal moment of the golden age, this original ground of
being—that indeed nevertheless has always endured and will
endure forever—there in the weekday of human existence, as
a tormenting thorn buried deeply in the soul, as a memorial
of a claim never fulfilled, as a fata morgana of a lost and
promised paradise; through this feverish dream "present" to a
condemned "past" in a clouded "future." I understood. This
inebriation was a space flight, not of the outer but rather of
the inner man, and for a moment I experienced reality from
a location that lies somewhere beyond the force of gravity of
time.

As I began again to feel this force of gravity, I was
childish enough to want to postpone the return by taking a
new dose of 6 mg psilocybin at 11:45, and once again 4 mg
at 14:30. The effect was trifling, and in any case not worth
mentioning.

Mrs. Li Gelpke, an artist, also participated in this series of
investigations, taking three self-experiments with LSD and
psilocybin. The artist wrote of the drawing she made during the
experiment:

Nothing on this page is consciously fashioned. While
I worked on it, the memory (of the experience under
psilocybin) was again reality, and led me at every stroke. For
that reason the picture is as many-layered as this memory,
and the figure at the lower right is really the captive of its
dream… When books about Mexican art came into my
hands three weeks later, I again found the motifs of my
visions there with a sudden start...

I have also mentioned the occurrence of Mexican motifs in
psilocybin inebriation during my first self-experiment with dried
Psilocybe mexicana mushrooms, as was described in the section
on the chemical investigation of these mushrooms. The same
phenomenon has also struck R. Gordon Wasson. Proceeding from
such observations, he has advanced the conjecture that ancient
Mexican art could have been influenced by visionary images, as
they appear in mushroom inebriation.

THE "MAGIC MORNING GLORY" OLOLIUHQUI

After we had managed to solve the riddle of the sacred
mushroom teonanacatl in a relatively short time, I also became
interested in the problem of another Mexican magic drug not yet
chemically elucidated, ololiuhqui. Ololiuhqui is the Aztec name
for the seeds of certain climbing plants (*Convolvulaceae*) that,
like the mescaline cactus peyotl and the teonanacatl mushrooms,
were used in pre-Columbian times by the Aztecs and neighboring

people in religious ceremonies and magical healing practices. Ololiuhqui is still used even today by certain Indian tribes like the Zapotec, Chinantec, Mazatec, and Mixtec, who until a short time ago still led a geniunely isolated existence, little influenced by Christianity, in the remote mountains of southern Mexico.

An excellent study of the historical, ethnological, and botanical aspects of ololiuhqui was published in 1941 by Richard Evans Schultes, director of the Harvard Botanical Museum in Cambridge, Massachusetts. It is entitled "A Contribution to Our Knowledge of *Rivea corymbosa*, the Narcotic Ololiuqui of the Aztecs." The following statements about the history of ololiuhqui derive chiefly from Schultes's monograph. [Translator's note: As R. Gordon Wasson has pointed out, "ololiuhqui" is a more precise orthography than the more popular spelling used by Schultes. See *Botanical Museum Leaflets* Harvard University 20: 161-212, 1963.]

The earliest records about this drug were written by Spanish chroniclers of the sixteenth century, who also mentioned peyotl and teonanacatl. Thus the Franciscan friar Bernardino de Sahagun, in his already cited famous chronicle *Historia General de las Cosas de Nueva Espana*, writes about the wondrous effects of ololiuhqui: "There is an herb, called *coatl xoxouhqui* (green snake), which produces seeds that are called ololiuhqui. These seeds stupefy and deprive one of reason: they are taken as a potion."

We obtain further information about these seeds from the physician Francisco Hernandez, whom Philip II sent to Mexico from Spain, from 1570 to 1575, in order to study the medicaments of the natives. In the chapter "On Ololiuhqui" of his monumental work entitled *Rerum Medicarum Novae Hispaniae Thesaurus seu Plantarum, Animalium Mineralium Mexicanorum Historia*, published in Rome in 1651, he gives a detailed description and the first illustration of ololiuhqui. An extract from the Latin text accompanying the illustration reads in translation: "Ololiuhqui, which others call *coaxihuitl* or snake plant, is a climber with thin, green, heart-shaped leaves... The flowers are white, fairly large...

The seeds are roundish... When the priests of the Indians wanted to visit with the gods and obtain information from them, they ate of this plant in order to become inebriated. Thousands of fantastic images and demons then appeared to them..." Despite this comparatively good description, the botanical identification of ololiuhqui as seeds of *Rivea corymbosa* (L.) Hall. f. occasioned many discussions in specialist circles. Recently preference has been given to the synonym *Turbina corymbosa* (L.) Raf.

When I decided in 1959 to attempt the isolation of the active principles of ololiuhqui, only a single report on chemical work with the seeds of *Turbina corymbosa* was available. It was the work of the pharmacologist C. G. Santesson of Stockholm, from the year 1937. Santesson, however, was not successful in isolating an active substance in pure form.

Contradictory findings had been published about the activity of theololiuhqui seeds. The psychiatrist H. Osmond conducted a self-experiment with the seeds of *Turbina corymbosa* in 1955. After the ingestion of 60 to 100 seeds, he entered into a state of apathy and emptiness, accompanied by enhanced visual sensitivity. After four hours, there followed a period of relaxation and well-being, lasting for a longer time. The results of V. J. Kinross-Wright, published in England in 1958, in which eight voluntary research subjects, who had taken up to 125 seeds, perceived no effects at all, contradicted this report.

Through the mediation of R. Gordon Wasson, I obtained two samples of ololiuhqui seeds. In his accompanying letter of 6 August 1959 from Mexico City, he wrote of them:

...The parcels that I am sending you are the following:

A small parcel of seeds that I take to be Rivea corymbosa, otherwise known as ololiuhqui well-known narcotic of the Aztecs, called in Huautla "la semilla de la Virgen." This parcel, you will find, consists of two little bottles, which represent two deliveries of seeds made to us in Huautla, and a larger batch of seeds delivered to us by

*Francisco Ortega "Chico," the Zapotec guide, who himself
gathered the seeds from the plants at the Zapotec town of
San Bartolo Yautepec...*

The first-named, round, light brown seeds from Huautla proved
in the botanical determination to have been correctly identified as
Rivea (Turbina) corymbosa, while the black, angular seeds from San
Bartolo Yautepec were identified as *Ipomoea violacea* L.

While *Turbina corymbosa* thrives only in tropical or subtropical
climates, one also finds *Ipomoea violacea* as an ornamental plant
dispersed over the whole earth in the temperate zones. It is the
morning glory that delights the eye in our gardens in diverse
varieties with blue or blue-red striped calyxes.

The Zapotec, besides the original ololiuhqui (that is, the seeds
of *Turbina corymbosa*, which they call *badoh*), also utilize *badoh
negro*, the seeds of *Ipomoea violacea*. T. MacDougall, who furnished
us with a second larger consignment of the last-named seeds,
made this observation.

My capable laboratory assistant Hans Tscherter, with whom
I had already carried out the isolation of the active principles of
the mushrooms, participated in the chemical investigation of the
ololiuhqui drug. We advanced the working hypothesis that the
active principles of the ololiuhqui seeds could be representatives
of the same class of chemical substances, the indole compounds, to
which LSD, psilocybin, and psilocin belong. Considering the very
great number of other groups of substances that, like the indoles,
were under consideration as active principles of ololiuhqui, it
was indeed extremely improbable that this assumption would
prove true. It could, however, very easily be tested. The presence
of indole compounds, of course, may simply and rapidly be
determined by colorimetric reactions. Thus even traces of indole
substances, with a certain reagent, give an intense blue-colored
solution.

We had luck with our hypothesis. Extracts of ololiuhqui
seeds with the appropriate reagent gave the blue coloration

characteristic of indole compounds. With the help of this colorimetric test, we succeeded in a short time in isolating the indole substances from the seeds and in obtaining them in chemically pure form. Their identification led to an astonishing result. What we found appeared at first scarcely believable. Only after repetition and the most careful scrutiny of the operations was our suspicion concerning the peculiar findings eliminated: the active principles from the ancient Mexican magic drug ololiuhqui proved to be identical with substances that were already present in my laboratory. They were identical with alkaloids that had been obtained in the course of the decades long investigations of ergot; partly isolated as such from ergot, partly obtained through chemical modification of ergot substances.

Lysergic acid amide, lysergic acid hydroxyethylamide, and alkaloids closely related to them chemically were established as the main active principles of ololiuhqui. (See formulae in the appendix.) Also present was the alkaloid ergobasine, whose synthesis had constituted the starting point of my investigations on ergot alkaloids. Lysergic acid amide and lysergic acid hydroxyethylamide, active principles of ololiuhqui, are chemically very closely related to lysergic acid diethylamide (LSD), which even for the nonchemist follows from the names.

Lysergic acid amide was described for the first time by the English chemists S. Smith and G. M. Timmis as a cleavage product of ergot alkaloids, and I had also produced this substance synthetically in the course of the investigations in which LSD originated. Certainly, nobody at the time could have suspected that this compound synthesized in the flask would be discovered twenty years later as a naturally occurring active principle of an ancient Mexican magic drug.

After the discovery of the psychic effects of LSD, I had also tested lysergic acid amide in a self-experiment and established that it likewise evoked a dreamlike condition, but only with about a tenfold to twentyfold greater dose than LSD. This effect was characterized by a sensation of mental emptiness and the unreality and meaninglessness of the outer world, by enhanced sensitivity of hearing, and by a not unpleasant physical lassitude, which ultimately led to sleep. This picture of the effects of LA-1 1 1, as lysergic acid amide was called as a research preparation, was confirmed in a systematic investigation by the psychiatrist Dr. H. Solms.

When I presented the findings of our investigations on ololiuhqui at the Natural Products Congress of the International Union for Pure and Applied Chemistry (IUPAC) in Sydney, Australia, in the fall of 1960, my colleagues received my talk with skepticism. In the discussions following my lecture, some persons voiced the suspicion that the ololiuhqui extracts could well have been contaminated with traces of lysergic acid derivatives, with which so much work had been done in my laboratory.

There was another reason for the doubt in specialist circles concerning our findings. The occurrence in higher plants (i.e., in the morning glory family) of ergot alkaloids that hitherto had been known only as constituents of lower fungi, contradicted the experience that certain substances are typical of and restricted to respective plant families. It is indeed a very rare exception to find a characteristic group of substances, in this case the ergot alkaloids, occurring in two divisions of the plant kingdom broadly separated in evolutionary history.

Our results were confirmed, however, when different laboratories in the United States, Germany, and Holland subsequently verified our investigations on the ololiuhqui seeds. Nevertheless, the skepticism went so far that some persons even considered the possibility that the seeds could have been infected with alkaloid-producing fungi. That suspicion, however, was ruled out experimentally.

These studies on the active principles of ololiuhqui seeds, although they were published only in professional journals, had an unexpected sequel. We were apprised by two Dutch wholesale seed companies that their sale of seeds of *Ipomoea violacea*, the ornamental blue morning glory, had reached unusual proportions in recent times. They had heard that the great demand was connected with investigations of these seeds in our laboratory, about which they were eager to learn the details. It turned out that the new demand derived from hippie circles and other groups interested in hallucinogenic drugs. They believed they had found in the ololiuhqui seeds a substitute for LSD, which was becoming less and less accessible.

The morning glory seed boom, however, lasted only a comparatively short time, evidently because of the undesirable experiences that those in the drug world had with this "new" ancient inebriant. The ololiuhqui seeds, which are taken crushed with water or another mild beverage, taste very bad and are difficult for the stomach to digest. Moreover, the psychic effects of ololiuhqui, in fact, differ from those of LSD in that the euphoric and the hallucinogenic components are less pronounced, while a sensation of mental emptiness, often anxiety and depression, predominates. Furthermore, weariness and lassitude are hardly desirable effects as traits in an inebriant. These could all be reasons why the drug culture's interest in the morning glory seeds has diminished.

Only a few investigations have considered the question whether the active principles of ololiuhqui could find a useful application in medicine. In my opinion, it would be worthwhile to clarify above all whether the strong narcotic, sedative effect of certain ololiuhqui constituents, or of chemical modifications of these, is medicinally useful.

My studies in the field of hallucinogenic drugs reached a kind of logical conclusion with the investigations of ololiuhqui. They now formed a circle, one could almost say a magic circle: the starting point had been the synthesis of lysergic acid amides, among them the naturally occurring ergot alkaloid ergobasin. This led to the synthesis of lysergic acid diethylamide, LSD.

The hallucinogenic properties of LSD were the reason why the hallucinogenic magic mushroom teonanacatl found its way into my laboratory. The work with teonanacatl, from which psilocybin and psilocin were isolated, proceeded to the investigation of another Mexican magic drug, ololiuhqui, in which hallucinogenic principles in the form of lysergic acid amides were again encountered, including ergobasine—with which the magic circle closed.

IN SEARCH OF THE MAGIC PLANT "SKA MARIA PASTORA" IN THE MAZATEC COUNTRY

R. Gordon Wasson, with whom I had maintained friendly relations since the investigations of the Mexican magic mushrooms, invited my wife and me to take part in an expedition to Mexico in the fall of 1962. The purpose of the journey was to search for another Mexican magic plant. Wasson had learned on his travels in the mountains of southern Mexico that the expressed juice of the leaves of a plant, which were called *hojas de la Pastora* or *hojas de Maria Pastora*, in Mazatec *ska Pastora* or *ska Maria Pastora* (leaves of the shepherdess or leaves of Mary the shepherdess), were used among the Mazatec in medico-religious practices, like the teonanacatl mushrooms and the ololiuhqui seeds.

The question now was to ascertain from what sort of plant the "leaves of Mary the shepherdess" derived, and then to identify this plant botanically. We also hoped, if at all possible, to gather sufficient plant material to conduct a chemical investigation on the hallucinogenic principles it contained.

RIDE THROUGH THE SIERRA MAZATECA

On 26 September 1962, my wife and I accordingly flew to Mexico City, where we met Gordon Wasson. He had made all the necessary preparations for the expedition, so that in two days we had already set out on the next leg of the journey to the south. Mrs. Irmgard Weitlaner Johnson (widow of Jean B. Johnson, a pioneer of the ethnographic study of the Mexican magic mushrooms, killed in the Allied landing in North Africa) had joined us. Her father, Robert J. Weitlaner, had emigrated to Mexico from Austria and had likewise contributed toward the rediscovery of the mushroom cult. Mrs. Johnson worked at the National Museum of Anthropology in Mexico City, as an expert on Indian textiles.

After a two-day journey in a spacious Land Rover, which took us over the plateau, along the snow-capped Popocatepetl, passing Puebla, down into the Valley of Orizaba with its magnificent tropical vegetation, then by ferry across the Popoloapan (Butterfly River), on through the former Aztec garrison Tuxtepec, we arrived at the starting point of our expedition, the Mazatec village of Jalapa de Diaz, lying on a hillside.

There we were in the midst of the environment and among the people that we would come to know in the succeeding 2 1/2 weeks.

There was an uproar upon our arrival in the marketplace, center of this village widely dispersed in the jungle. Old and young men, who had been squatting and standing around in the half-opened bars and shops, pressed suspiciously yet curiously about our Land Rover; they were mostly barefoot but all wore a sombrero. Women and girls were nowhere to be seen. One of the men gave us to understand that we should follow him. He led us to the local president, a fat mestizo who had his office in a one-story house with a corrugated iron roof. Gordon showed him our credentials from the civil authorities and from the military governor of Oaxaca, which explained that we had come here to carry out scientific investigations. The president, who probably could not read at all, was visibly impressed by the large-sized documents equipped with official seals. He had lodgings assigned to us in a spacious shed, in which we could place our air mattresses and sleeping bags.

I looked around the region somewhat. The ruins of a large church from colonial times, which must have once been very beautiful, rose almost ghostlike in the direction of an ascending slope at the side of the village square. Now I could also see women looking out of their huts, venturing to examine the strangers. In their long, white dresses, adorned with red borders, and with their long braids of blue-black hair, they offered a picturesque sight.

We were fed by an old Mazatec woman, who directed a young cook and two helpers. She lived in one of the typical Mazatec huts. These are simply rectangular structures with thatched gabled roofs and walls of wooden poles joined together, windowless, the chinks between the wooden poles offering sufficient opportunity to look out. In the middle of the hut, on the stamped clay floor, was an elevated, open fireplace, built up out of dried clay or made of stones. The smoke escaped through large openings in the walls under the two ends of the roof. Bast mats that lay in a corner or along the walls served as beds. The huts were shared with the domestic animals, as well as black swine, turkeys, and chickens. There was roasted chicken to eat, black beans, and also, in place of bread, tortillas, a type of cornmeal pancake that is baked on the hot stone slab of the hearth. Beer and tequila, an Agave liquor, were served.

Next morning our troop formed for the ride through the Sierra Mazateca. Mules and guides were engaged from the horsekeeper of the village. Guadelupe, the Mazatec familiar with the route, took charge of guiding the lead animal. Gordon, Irmgard, my wife, and I were stationed on our mules in the middle. Teodosio and Pedro, called Chico, two young fellows who trotted along barefoot beside the two mules laden with our baggage, brought up the rear.

It took some time to get accustomed to the hard wooden saddles. Then, however, this mode of locomotion proved to be the most ideal type of travel that I know of. The mules followed the leader, single file, at a steady pace. They required no direction at all by the rider. With surprising dexterity, they sought out the best spots along the almost impassable, partly rocky, partly marshy paths, which led through thickets and streams or onto precipitous slopes. Relieved of all travel cares, we could devote all our attention to the beauty of the landscape and the tropical vegetation. There were tropical forests with gigantic trees overgrown with twining plants, then again clearings with banana groves or coffee plantations, between light stands of trees, flowers at the edge of the path, over which wondrous butterflies bustled about... We made our way upstream along the broad riverbed of Rio Santo Domingo, with brooding heat and steamy air, now steeply ascending, then again falling. During a short, violent tropical downpour, the long broad ponchos of oilcloth, with which Gordon had equipped us, proved quite useful. Our Indian guides had protected themselves from the cloudburst with gigantic, heart-shaped leaves that they nimbly chopped off at the edge of the path. Teodosio and Chico gave the impression of great, green hay ricks as they ran, covered with these leaves, beside their mules.

Shortly before nightfall we arrived at the first settlement, La Providencia ranch. The patron, Don Joaquin Garcia, the head of a large family, welcomed us hospitably and full of dignity. It was impossible to determine how many children, in addition to the grown-ups and the domestic animals, were present in the large living room, feebly illuminated by the hearth fire alone.

Gordon and I placed our sleeping bags outdoors under the projecting roof. I awoke in the morning to find a pig grunting over my face.

After another day's journey on the backs of our worthy mules, we arrived at Ayautla, a Mazatec settlement spread across a hillside. En route, among the shrubbery, I had delighted in the blue calyxes of the magic morning glory *Ipomoea violacea*, the mother plant of the ololiuhqui seeds. It grew wild there, whereas among us it is only found in the garden as an ornamental plant.

We remained in Ayautla for several days. We had lodging in the house of Dona Donata Sosa de Garcia. Dona Donata was in charge of a large family, which included her ailing husband. In addition, she presided over the coffee cultivation of the region. The collection center for the freshly picked coffee beans was in an adjacent building. It was a lovely picture, the young Indian woman and girls returning home from the harvest toward evening, in their bright garments adorned with colored borders, the coffee sacks carried on their backs by headbands. Dona Donata also managed a type of grocery store, in which her husband, Don Eduardo, stood behind the counter.

In the evening by candlelight, Dona Donata, who besides Mazatec also spoke Spanish, told us about life in the village; one tragedy or another had already struck nearly every one of the seemingly peaceful huts that lay surrounded by this paradisiacal scenery. A man who had murdered his wife, and who now sits in prison for life, had lived in the house next door, which now stood empty. The husband of a daughter of Dona Donata, after an affair with another woman, was murdered out of jealousy. The president of Ayautla, a young bull of a mestizo, to whom we had made our formal visit in the afternoon, never made the short walk from his hut to his "office" in the village hall (with the corrugated iron roof) unless accompanied by two heavily armed men. Because he exacted illegal taxes, he was afraid of being shot to death. Since no higher authority sees to justice in this remote region, people have recourse to self-defense of this type.

Thanks to Dona Donata's good connections, we received the first sample of the sought-after plant, some leaves of hojas de la Pastora, from an old woman. Since the flowers and roots were missing, however, this plant material was not suitable for botanical identification. Our efforts to obtain more precise information about the habitat of the plant and its use were also fruitless.

The continuation of our journey from Ayautla was delayed, as we had to wait until our boys could again bring back the mules that they had taken to pasture on the other side of Rio Santo Domingo, over the river swollen by intense downpours.

After a two-day ride, on which we had passed the night in the high mountain village of San Miguel Huautla, we arrived at Rio Santiago. Here we were joined by Dona Herlinda Martinez Cid, a teacher from Huautla de Jimenez. She had ridden over on the invitation of Gordon Wasson, who had known her since his mushroom expeditions, and was to serve as our Mazatec and Spanish-speaking interpreter. Moreover, she could help us, through her numerous relatives scattered in the region, to pave the way to contacts with curanderos and curanderas who used the hojas de la Pastora in their practice. Because of our delayed arrival in Rio Santiago, Dona Herlinda, who was acquainted with the dangers of the region, had been apprehensive about us, fearing we might have plunged down a rocky path or been attacked by robbers.

Our next stop was in San Jose Tenango, a settlement lying deep in a valley, in the midst of tropical vegetation with orange and lemon trees and banana plantations. Here again was the typical village picture: in the center, a marketplace with a half-ruined church from the colonial period, with two or three stands, a general store, and shelters for horses and mules. We found lodging in corrugated iron barracks, with the special luxury of a cement floor, on which we could spread out our sleeping bags.

In the thick jungle on the mountainside we discovered a spring, whose magnificent fresh water in a natural rocky basin invited us to bathe. That was an unforgettable pleasure after days without opportunities to wash properly. In this grotto I saw a hummingbird for the first time in nature, a blue-green, metallic, iridescent gem, which whirred over great liana blossoms.

The desired contact with persons skilled in medicine came about thanks to the kindred connections of Dona Herlinda, beginning with the curandero Don Sabino. But he refused, for some reason, to receive us in a consultation and to question the leaves. From an old curandera, a venerable woman in a strikingly magnificent Mazatec garment, with the lovely name Natividad Rosa, we received a whole bundle of flowering specimens of the sought-after plant, but even she could not be prevailed upon to perform a ceremony with the leaves for us. Her excuse was that she was too old for the hardship of the magical trip; she could never cover the long distance to certain places: a spring where the wise women gather their powers, a lake on which the sparrows sing, and where objects get their names. Nor would Natividad Rosa tell us where she had gathered the leaves. They grew in a very, very distant forest valley. Wherever she dug up a plant, she put a coffee bean in the earth as thanks to the gods.

We now possessed ample plants with flowers and roots, which were suitable for botanical identification. It was apparently a representative of the genus *Salvia*, a relative of the well-known meadow sage. The plants had blue flowers crowned with a white dome, which are arranged on a panicle 20 to 30 cm long, whose stem leaked blue.

Several days later, Natividad Rosa brought us a whole basket of leaves, for which she was paid fifty pesos. The business seemed to have been discussed, for two other women brought us further quantities of leaves. As it was known that the expressed juice of the leaves is drunk in the ceremony, and this must therefore contain the active principle, the fresh leaves were crushed on a stone plate, squeezed out in a cloth, the juice diluted with alcohol as a preservative, and decanted into flasks in order to be studied later in the laboratory in Basel. I was assisted in this work by an Indian girl, who was accustomed to dealing with the stone plate, the *metate*, on which the Indians since ancient times have ground their corn by hand.

On the day before the journey was to continue, having given up all hope of being able to attend a ceremony, we suddenly made another contact with a curandera, one who was ready "to serve us." A confidante of Herlinda's, who had produced this contact, led us after nightfall along a secret path to the hut of the curandera, lying solitary on the mountainside above the settlement. No one from the village was to see us or discover that we were received there. It was obviously considered a betrayal of sacred customs, worthy of punishment, to allow strangers, whites, to take part in this. That indeed had also been the real reason why the other healers whom we asked had refused to admit us to a leaf ceremony. Strange birdcalls from the darkness accompanied us on the ascent, and the barking of dogs was heard on all sides. The dogs had detected the strangers. The curandera Consuela Garcia, a woman of some forty years, barefoot like all Indian women in this region, timidly admitted us to her hut and immediately closed up the doorway with a heavy bar. She bid us lie down on the bast mats on the stamped mud floor. As Consuela spoke only Mazatec, Herlinda translated her instructions into Spanish for us. The curandera lit a candle on a table covered with some images of saints, along with a variety of rubbish. Then she began to bustle about busily, but in silence. All at once we heard peculiar noises and a rummaging in the room—did the hut harbor some hidden person whose shape and proportions could not be made out in the candlelight? Visibly disturbed, Consuela searched the room with the burning candle. It appeared to be merely rats, however, who were working their mischief. In a bowl the curandera now kindled copal, an incense-like resin, which soon filled the whole hut with its aroma. Then the magic potion was ceremoniously prepared. Consuela inquired which of us wished to drink of it with her. Gordon announced himself. Since I was suffering from a severe stomach upset at the time, I could not join in. My wife substituted for me. The curandera laid out six pairs of leaves for herself. She apportioned the same number to Gordon. Anita received three pairs. Like the mushrooms, the leaves are always dosed in pairs, a practice that, of course, has a magical significance. The leaves were crushed with the metate, then squeezed out through a fine sieve into a cup, and the metate and the contents of the sieve were rinsed with water. Finally, the filled cups were incensed over the copal vessel with much ceremony. Consuela asked Anita and Gordon, before she handed them their cups, whether they believed in the truth and the holiness of the ceremony. After they answered in the affirmative and the very bitter-tasting potion was solemnly imbibed, the candles were extinguished and, lying in darkness on the bast masts, we awaited the effects.

After some twenty minutes Anita whispered to me that she saw striking, brightly bordered images. Gordon also perceived the effect of the drug. The voice of the curandera sounded from the darkness, half speaking, half singing. Herlinda translated: Did we believe in Christ's blood and the holiness of the rites? After our "creemos" ("We believe"), the ceremonial performance continued. The curandera lit the candles, moved them from the altar table onto the floor, sang and spoke prayers or magic formulas, placed the candles again under the images of the saints—then again silence and darkness. Thereupon the true consultation began. Consuela asked for our request. Gordon inquired after the health of his daughter, who immediately before his departure from New York had to be admitted prematurely to the hospital in expectation of a baby. He received the comforting information that mother and child were well. Then again came singing and prayer and manipulations with the candles on the altar table and on the floor, over the smoking basin.

When the ceremony was at an end, the curandera asked us to rest yet a while longer in prayer on our bast mats. Suddenly a thunderstorm burst out. Through the cracks of the beam walls, lightning flashed into the darkness of the hut, accompanied by violent thunderbolts, while a tropical downpour raged, beating on the roof. Consuela voiced apprehension that we would not be able to leave her house unseen in the darkness. But the thunderstorm let up before daybreak, and we went down the mountainside to our corrugated iron barracks, as noiselessly as possible by the light of flashlights, unnoticed by the villagers, but dogs again barked from all sides.

Participation in this ceremony was the climax of our expedition. It brought confirmation that the hojas de la Pastora were used by the Indians for the same purpose and in the same ceremonial milieu as teonanacatl, the sacred mushrooms. Now we also had authentic plant material, not only sufficient for botanical identification, but also for the planned chemical analysis. The inebriated state that Gordon Wasson and my wife had experienced with the hojas had been shallow and only of short duration, yet it had exhibited a distinctly hallucinogenic character.

On the morning after this eventful night we took leave of San Jose Tenango. The guide, Guadelupe, and the two fellows Teodosio and Pedro appeared before our barracks with the mules at the appointed time. Soon packed up and mounted, our little troop then moved uphill again, through the fertile landscape glittering in the sunlight from the night's thunderstorm. Returning by way of Santiago, toward evening we reached our last stop in Mazatec country, the capital Huautla de Jimenez.

From here on, the return trip to Mexico City was made by automobile. With a final supper in the Posada Rosaura, at the time the only inn in Huautla, we took leave of our Indian guides and of the worthy mules that had carried us so surefootedly and in such a pleasant way through the Sierra Mazatec. The Indians were paid off, and Teodosio, who also accepted payment for his chief in Jalapa de Diaz (where the animals were to be returned afterward), gave a receipt with his thumbprint colored by a ballpoint pen. We took up quarters in Dona Herlinda's house.

A day later we made our formal visit to the curandera Maria Sabina, a woman made famous by the Wassons' publications. It had been in her hut that Gordon Wasson became the first white man to taste of the sacred mushrooms, in the course of a nocturnal ceremony in the summer of 1955. Gordon and Maria Sabina greeted each other cordially, as old friends. The curandera lived out of the way, on the mountainside above Huautla. The house in which the historic session with Gordon Wasson had taken place had been burned, presumably by angered residents or an envious colleague, because she had divulged the secret of teonanacatl to strangers. In the new hut in which we found ourselves, an incredible disorder prevailed, as had probably also prevailed in the old hut, in which half-naked children, hens, and pigs bustled about. The old curandera had an intelligent face, exceptionally changeable in expression. She was obviously impressed when it was explained that we had managed to confine the spirit of the mushrooms in pills, and she at once declared herself ready to "serve us" with these, that is, to grant us a consultation. It was agreed that this should take place the coming night in the house of Dona Herlinda.

In the course of the day I took a stroll through Huautla de Jimenez, which led along a main street on the mountainside. Then I accompanied Gordon on his visit to the Instituto Nacional Indigenista. This governmental organization had the duty of studying and helping to solve the problems of the indigenous population, that is, the Indians. Its leader told us of the difficulties that the "coffee policy" had caused in the area at that time. The president of Huautla, in collaboration with the Instituto Nacional Indigenista had tried to eliminate middlemen in order to shape the coffee prices favorably for the producing Indians. His body was found, mutilated, the previous June.

Our stroll also took us past the cathedral, from which Gregorian chants resounded. Old Father Aragon, whom Gordon knew well from his earlier stays, invited us into the vestry for a glass of tequila.

A MUSHROOM CEREMONY

As we returned home to Herlinda's house toward evening,

Maria Sabina had already arrived there with a large company, her two lovely daughters, Apolonia and Aurora (two prospective curanderas), and a niece, all of whom brought children along with them. Whenever her child began to cry, Apolonia would offer her breast to it. The old curandero Don Aurelio also appeared, a mighty man, one-eyed, in a black-and-white patterned *serape* (cloak). Cacao and sweet pastry were served on the veranda. I was reminded of the report from an ancient chronicle which described how *chocotatl* was drunk before the ingestion of teonanacatl.

After the fall of darkness, we all proceeded into the room in which the ceremony would take place. It was then locked up— that is, the door was obstructed with the only bed available. Only an emergency exit into the back garden remained unlatched for absolute necessity. It was nearly midnight when the ceremony began. Until that time the whole party lay, in darkness sleeping or awaiting the night's events, on the bast mats spread on the floor. Maria Sabina threw a piece of copal on the embers of a brazier from time to time, whereby the stuffy air in the crowded room became somewhat bearable. I had explained to the curandera through Herlinda, who was again with the party as interpreter, that one pill contained the spirit of two pairs of mushrooms. (The pills contained 5.0 mg synthetic psilocybin apiece.)

When all was ready, Maria Sabina apportioned the pills in pairs among the grown-ups present. After solemn smoking, she herself took two pairs (corresponding to 20 mg psilocybin). She gave the same dose to Don Aurelio and her daughter Apolonia, who would also serve as curandera. Aurora received one pair, as did Gordon, while my wife and Irmgard got only one pill each.

One of the children, a girl of about ten, under the guidance of Maria Sabina, had prepared for me the juice of five pairs of fresh leaves of hojas de la Pastora. I wanted to experience this drug that I had been unable to try in San Jose Tenango. The potion was said to be especially active when prepared by an innocent child. The cup with the expressed juice was likewise incensed and blessed by

Maria Sabina and Don Aurelio, before it was delivered to me.

All of these preparations and the following ceremony progressed in much the same way as the consultation with the curandera Consuela Garcia in San Jose Tenango.

After the drug was apportioned and the candle on the altar was extinguished, we awaited the effects in the darkness.

Before a half hour had elapsed, the curandera murmured something; her daughter and Don Aurelio also became restless. Herlinda translated and explained to us what was wrong. Maria Sabina had said that the pills lacked the spirit of the mushrooms. I discussed the situation with Gordon, who lay beside me. For us it was clear that absorption of the active principle from the pills, which must first dissolve in the stomach, occurs more slowly than from the mushrooms, in which some of the active principle already becomes absorbed through the mucous membranes during chewing. But how could we give a scientific explanation under such conditions? Rather than try to explain, we decided to act. We distributed more pills. Both curanderas and the curandero each received another pair. They had now each taken a total dosage of 30 mg psilocybin.

After about another quarter of an hour, the spirit of the pills did begin to yield its effects, which lasted until the crack of dawn. The daughters, and Don Aurelio with his deep bass voice, fervently answered the prayers and singing of the curandera. Blissful, yearning moans of Apolonia and Aurora, between singing and prayer, gave the impression that the religious experience of the young women in the drug inebriation was combined with sensual-sexual feelings.

In the middle of the ceremony Maria Sabina asked for our request. Gordon inquired again after the health of his daughter and grandchild. He received the same good information as from the curandera Consuela. Mother and child were in fact well when he returned home to New York. Obviously, however, this still represents no proof of the prophetic abilities of both curanderas.

Evidently as an effect of the hojas, I found myself for some time in a state of mental sensitivity and intense experience, which, however, was not accompanied by hallucinations. Anita, Irmgard, and Gordon experienced a euphoric condition of inebriation that was influenced by the strange, mystical atmosphere. My wife was impressed by the vision of very distinct strange line patterns.

She was astonished and perplexed, later, on discovering precisely the same images in the rich ornamentation over the altar in an old church near Puebla. That was on the return trip to Mexico City, when we visited churches from colonial times. These admirable churches offer great cultural and historical interest because the Indian artists and workmen who assisted in their construction smuggled in elements of Indian style. Klaus Thomas, in his book *Die kunstlich gesteuerte Seele* [The artificially steered mind] (Ferdinand Enke Verlag, Stuttgart, 1970), writes about the possible influence of visions from psilocybin inebriation on Meso-American Indian art: "Surely a cultural/historical comparison of the old and new creations of Indian art ... must convince the unbiased spectator of the harmony with the images, forms and colors of a psilocybin inebriation." The Mexican character of the visions seen in my first experience with dried *Psilocybe mexicana* mushrooms and the drawing of Li Gelpke after a psilocybin inebriation could also point to such an association.

As we took leave of Maria Sabina and her clan at the crack of dawn, the curandera said that the pills had the same power as the mushrooms, that there was no difference. This was a confirmation from the most competent authority, that the synthetic psilocybin is identical with the natural product. As a parting gift I let Maria Sabina have a vial of psilocybin pills. She radiantly explained to our interpreter Herlinda that she could now give consultations even in the season when no mushrooms grow.

How should we judge the conduct of Maria Sabina, the fact that she allowed strangers, white people, access to the secret ceremony, and let them try the sacred mushroom?

To her credit it can be said that she had thereby opened the door to the exploration of the Mexican mushroom cult in its present form, and to the scientific, botanical, and chemical investigation of the sacred mushrooms. Valuable active substances, psilocybin and psilocin, resulted. Without this assistance, the ancient knowledge and experience that was concealed in these secret practices would possibly, even probably, have disappeared without a trace, without having borne fruit, in the advancement of Western civilization.

From another standpoint, the conduct of this curandera can be regarded as a profanation of a sacred custom—even as a betrayal. Some of her countrymen were of this opinion, which was expressed in acts of revenge, including the burning of her house.

The profanation of the mushroom cult did not stop with the scientific investigations. The publication about the magic mushrooms unleashed an invasion of hippies and drug seekers into the Mazatec country, many of whom behaved badly, some even criminally. Another undesirable consequence was the beginning of true tourism in Huautla de Jimenez, whereby the originality of the place was eradicated.

Such statements and considerations are, for the most part, the concern of ethnographic research. Wherever researchers and scientists trace and elucidate the remains of ancient customs that are becoming rarer, their primitiveness is lost. This loss is only more or less counterbalanced when the outcome of the research represents a lasting cultural gain.

From Huautla de Jimenez we proceeded first to Teotitlan, in a breakneck truck ride along a half-paved road, and from there went on a comfortable car trip back to Mexico City, the starting point of our expedition. I had lost several kilograms in body weight, but was overwhelmingly compensated in enchanting experiences.

The herbarium samples of hojas de la Pastora, which we had brought with us, were subjected to botanical indentification by Carl Epling and Carlos D. Jativa at the Botanical Institute of

Harvard University in Cambridge, Massachusetts. They found
that this plant was a hitherto undescribed species of *Salvia*, which
was named *Salvia divinorum* by these authors. The chemical
investigation of the juice of the magic sage in the laboratory in
Basel was unsuccessful. The psychoactive principle of this drug
seems to be a rather unstable substance, since the juice prepared
in Mexico and preserved with alcohol proved in self-experiments
to be no longer active. Where the chemical nature of the active
principle is concerned, the problem of the magic plant ska Maria
Pastora still awaits solution. [Publisher's note: In 2002, Roth et
al. found that Salvinorin A., the active principle in ska Maria,
is a kappa-opiod receptor agonist, making it pharmacologically
distinct from LSD and other psychedelics, which primarily affect
serotonin receptors.]

So far in this book I have mainly described my scientific work
and matters relating to my professional activity. But this work, by
its very nature, had repercussions on my own life and personality,
not least because it brought me into contact with interesting
and important contemporaries. I have already mentioned some
of them—Timothy Leary, Rudolf Gelpke, Gordon Wasson.
Now, in the pages that follow, I would like to emerge from the
natural scientist's reserve, in order to portray encounters which
were personally meaningful to me and which helped me solve
questions posed by the substances I had discovered.

Chapter 7
Radiance from Ernst Jünger

RADIANCE IS THE PERFECT TERM to express the influence that
Ernst Jünger's literary work and personality have had on me.
In the light of his perspective, which stereoscopically comprises
the surfaces and depths of things, the world I knew took on a
new, translucent splendor. That happened a long time before the
discovery of LSD and before I came into personal contact with
this author in connection with hallucinogenic drugs.

My enchantment with Ernst Jünger began with his book *Das
Abenteuerliche Herz* [The adventurous heart]. Again and again in
the last forty years I have taken up this book. Here more than
ever, in themes that weigh more lightly and lie closer to me than
war and a new type of human being (subjects of Jünger's earlier
books), the beauty and magic of Jünger's prose was opened
to me—descriptions of flowers, of dreams, of solitary walks;
thoughts about chance, the future, colors, and about other themes
that have direct relation to our personal lives. Everywhere in
his prose the miracle of creation became evident, in the precise
description of the surfaces and, in translucence, of the depths; and
the uniqueness and the imperishable in every human being was
touched upon. No other writer has thus opened my eyes.

Drugs were also mentioned in *Das Abenteuerliche Herz*. Many
years passed, however, before I myself began to be especially
interested in this subject, after the discovery of the psychic effects
of LSD.

My first correspondence with Ernst Jünger had nothing to
do with the context of drugs; rather I once wrote to him on his

birthday, as a thankful reader.

Bottmingen, 29 March 1947

Dear Mr. Jünger,

As one richly endowed by you for years, I wished to send a jar of honey to you for your birthday. But I did not have this pleasure, because my export license has been refused in Bern.

The gift was intended less as a greeting from a country in which milk and honey still flow, than as a reminiscence of the enchanting sentences in your book AUF DEN MARMORKLIPPEN (ON THE MARBLE CLIFFS), where you speak of the "golden bees."

The book mentioned here had appeared in 1939, just shortly before the outbreak of World War II. *Auf den Marmorklippen* is not only a masterpiece of German prose, but also a work of great significance because in this book the characteristics of tyrants and the horror of war and nocturnal bombardment are described prophetically, in poetic vision.

In the course of our correspondence, Ernst Jünger also inquired about my LSD studies, of which he had learned through a friend. Thereupon I sent him the pertinent publications, which he acknowledged with the following comments:

Kirchhorst, 3/3/1948

...together with both enclosures concerning your new phantasticum. It seems indeed that you have entered a field that contains so many tempting mysteries.

Your consignment came together with the CONFESSIONS OF AN ENGLISH OPIUM EATER, that has just been published in a new translation. The translator writes me that his reading of DAS ABENTEUERLICHE HERZ stimulated him to do his work.

As far as I am concerned, my practical studies in this field are far behind me. These are experiments in which one sooner or later embarks on truly dangerous paths, and may be considered lucky to escape with only a black eye.

What interested me above all was the relationship of these substances to productivity. It has been my experience, however, that creative achievement requires an alert consciousness, and that it diminishes under the spell of drugs. On the other hand, conceptualization is important, and one gains insights under the influence of drugs that indeed are not possible otherwise. I consider the beautiful essay that Maupassant has written about ether to be such an insight. Moreover, I had the impression that in fever one also discovers new landscapes, new archipelagos, and a new music, that becomes completely distinct when the "customs station" ["An der Zollstation" [At the custom station], the title heading of a section in DAS ABENTEUERLICHE HERZ (2d ed.) that concerns the transition from life to death.] appears. For geographic description, on the other hand, one must be fully conscious. What productivity means to the artist, healing means to the physician. Accordingly, it also may suffice for him that he sometimes enters the regions through the tapestries that our senses have woven. Moreover, I seem to perceive in our time less of a taste for the phantastica than for the energetica—amphetamine, which has even been furnished to fliers and other soldiers by the armies, belongs to this group. Tea is in my opinion a phantasticum, coffee an energeticum—tea therefore possesses a disproportionately higher artistic rank. I notice that coffee disrupts the delicate lattice of light and shadows, the fruitful doubts that emerge during the writing of a sentence. One exceeds his inhibitions. With tea, on the other hand, the thoughts climb genuinely upward.

So far as my "studies" are concerned, I had a manuscript on that topic, but have since burned it. My excursions terminated with hashish that led to very pleasant, but also to manic states, to Oriental tyranny...

Soon afterward, in a letter from Ernst Jünger I learned that he had inserted a discourse about drugs in the novel *Heliopolis*, on which he was then working. He wrote to me about the drug researcher who figures in the novel:

> *Among the trips in the geographical and metaphysical worlds, which I am attempting to describe there, are those of a purely sedentary man, who explores the archipelagos beyond the navigable seas, for which he uses drugs as a vehicle. I give extracts from his log book. Certainly, I cannot allow this Columbus of the inner globe to end well—he dies of a poisoning. Avis au lecteur.*

The book that appeared the following year bore the subtitle *Ruckblick auf eine Stadt* [Retrospective on a city], a retrospective on a city of the future, in which technical apparatus and the weapons of the present time were developed still further in magic, and in which power struggles between a demonic technocracy and a conservative force took place. In the figure of Antonio Peri, Jünger depicted the mentioned drug researcher, who resided in the ancient city of *Heliopolis*.

> *He captured dreams, just like others appear to chase after butterflies with nets. He did not travel to the islands on Sundays and holidays and did not frequent the taverns on Pagos Beach. He locked himself up in his studio for trips into the dreamy regions. He said that all countries and unknown islands were woven into the tapestry. The drugs served him as keys to entry into the chambers and caves of this world. In the course of the years he had gained great knowledge, and he kept a log book of his excursions. A small library adjoined this studio, consisting partly of herbals and medicinal reports, partly of works by poets and magicians. Antonio tended to read there while the effect of the drug itself developed... He went on voyages of discovery in the universe of his brain...*

In the center of this library, which was pillaged by mercenaries of the provincial governor during the arrest of Antonio Peri, stood

> The great inspirers of the nineteenth century: De
> Quincey, E.T.A. Hoffmann, Poe, and Baudelaire. Yet there
> were also books from the ancient past: herbals, necromancy
> texts, and demonology of the middle-aged world. They
> included the names Albertus Magnus, Raimundus Lullus,
> and Agrippa of Nettesheym... Moreover, there was the great
> folio DE PRAESTIGIIS DAEMONUM by Wierus, and the very
> unique compilations of Medicus Weckerus, published in
> Basel in 1582...

In another part of his collection, Antonio Peri seemed to have cast his attention principally "on ancient pharmacology books, formularies and pharmacopoeias, and to have hunted for reprints of journals and annals. Among others was found a heavy old volume by the Heidelberg psychologists on the extract of mescal buttons, and a paper on the phantastica of ergot by Hofmann-Bottmingen..."

In the same year in which Heliopolis came out, I made the personal acquaintance of the author. I went to meet Ernst Jünger in Ravensburg, for a Swiss sojourn. On a wonderful fall journey in southern Switzerland, together with mutual friends, I experienced the radiant power of his personality.

Two years later, at the beginning of February 1951, came the great adventure, an LSD trip with Ernst Jünger. Since, up until that moment, there were only reports of LSD experiments in connection with psychiatric inquiries, this experiment especially interested me, because this was an opportunity to observe the effects of LSD on the artistic person, in a nonmedical milieu. That was still somewhat before Aldous Huxley, from the same perspective, began to experiment with mescaline, about which he then reported in his two books The Doors of Perception and Heaven and Hell.

In order to have medical aid on hand if necessary, I invited my friend, the physician and pharmacologist Professor Heribert

Konzett, to participate. The trip took place at 10:00 in the morning, in the living room of our house in Bottmingen. Since the reaction of such a highly sensitive man as Ernst Jünger was not foreseeable, a low dose was chosen for this first experiment as a precaution, only 0.05 mg. The experiment, then, did not lead into great depths.

The beginning phase was characterized by the intensification of aesthetic experience. Red-violet roses were of unknown luminosity and radiated in portentous brightness. The concerto for flute and harp by Mozart was perceived in its celestial beauty as heavenly music. In mutual astonishment we contemplated the haze of smoke that ascended with the ease of thought from a Japanese incense stick. As the inebriation became deeper and the conversation ended, we came to fantastic reveries while we lay in our easy chairs with closed eyes. Ernst Jünger enjoyed the color display of Oriental images; I was on a trip among Berber tribes in North Africa, saw colored caravans and lush oases. Heribert Konzett, whose features seemed to me to be transfigured, Buddha-like, experienced a breath of timelessness, liberation from the past and the future, blessedness through being completely here and now.

The return from the altered state of consciousness was associated with strong sensitivity to cold. Like freezing travelers, we enveloped ourselves in covers for the landing. The return to everyday reality was celebrated with a good dinner, in which Burgundy flowed copiously.

This trip was characterized by the mutuality and parallelism of our experiences, which were perceived as profoundly joyful. All three of us had drawn near the gate to an experience of mystical being; however, it did not open. The dose we had chosen was too low. In misunderstanding this reason, Ernst Jünger, who had earlier been thrust into deeper realms by a high dose of mescaline, remarked: "Compared with the tiger mescaline, your LSD, is, after all, only a house cat." After later experiments with higher doses of

LSD, he revised this estimation.

Jünger has assimilated the mentioned spectacle of the incense stick into literature, in his story *Besuch auf Gotenhotm* [Visit to Godenholm], in which deeper experiences of drug inebriation also play a part:

> *Schwarzenberg burned an incense stick, as he sometimes did, to clear the air. A blue plume ascended from the tip of the stick. Moltner looked at it first with astonishment, then with delight, as if a new power of the eyes had come to him. It revealed itself in the play of this fragrant smoke, which ascended from the slender stick and then branched out into a delicate crown. It was as if his imagination had created it—a pallid web of sea lilies in the depths, that scarcely trembled from the beat of the surf. Time was active in this creation—it had circled it, whirled about it, wreathed it, as if imaginary coins rapidly piled up one on top of another. The abundance of space revealed itself in the fiber work, the nerves, which stretched and unfolded in the height, in a vast number of filaments.*
>
> *Now a breath of air affected the vision, and softly twisted it about the shaft like a dancer. Moltner uttered a shout of surprise. The beams and lattices of the wondrous flower wheeled around in new planes, in new fields. Myriads of molecules observed the harmony. Here the laws no longer acted under the veil of appearance; matter was so delicate and weightless that it clearly reflected them. How simple and cogent everything was. The numbers, masses and weights stood out from matter. They cast off the raiments. No goddess could inform the initiates more boldly and freely. The pyramids with their weight did not reach up to this revelation. That was Pythagorean luster. No spectacle had ever affected him with such a magic spell.*

This deepened experience in the aesthetic sphere, as it is described here in the example of contemplation of a haze of blue smoke, is typical of the beginning phase of LSD inebriation, before deeper alterations of conscious begin.

I visited Ernst Jünger occasionally in the following years, in Wilfingen, Germany, where he had moved from Ravensburg, or we met in Switzerland, at my place in Bottmingen, or in Bundnerland in southeastern Switzerland. Through the shared LSD experience, our relations had deepened. Drugs and problems connected with them constituted a major subject of our conversation and correspondence, without our having made further practical experiments in the meantime.

We exchanged literature about drugs. Ernst Jünger thus let me have for my drug library the rare, valuable monograph of Dr. Ernst Freiherrn von Bibra, *Die Narkotischen Genussmittel und der Mensch* [Narcotic pleasure drugs and man] printed in Nuremburg in 1855. This book is a pioneering, standard work of drug literature, a source of the first order, above all as relates to the history of drugs. What von Bibra embraces under the designation "Narkotischen Genussmittel" are not only substances like opium and thorn apple, but also coffee, tobacco, khat, which do not fall under the present conception of narcotics, any more than do drugs such as coca, fly agaric, and hashish, which he also described.

Noteworthy, and today still as topical as at the time, are the general opinions about drugs that von Bibra contrived more than a century ago:

> *The individual who has taken too much hashish, and then runs frantically about in the streets and attacks everyone who confronts him, sinks into insignificance beside the numbers of those who after mealtime pass calm and happy hours with a moderate dose; and the number of those who are able to overcome the heaviest exertions through coca, yes, who were possibly rescued from death by starvation through coca, by far exceed the few coqueros who have undermined their health by immoderate use. In the*

same manner, only a misplaced hypocrisy can condemn the
vinous cup of old father Noah, because individual drunkards
do not know how to observe limit and moderation.

From time to time I advised Ernst Jünger about actual and
entertaining events in the field of inebriating drugs, as in my
letter of September 1955:

>*...Last week the first 200 grams of a new drug arrived,*
>*whose investigation I wish to take up. It involves the seeds*
>*of a mimosa (Piptadenia peregrina Benth.) that is used*
>*as a stimulating intoxicant by the Indians of the Orinoco.*
>*The seeds are ground, fermented, and then mixed with*
>*the powder of burned snail shells. This powder is sniffed*
>*by the Indians with the help of a hollow, forked bird bone,*
>*as already reported by Alexander von Humboldt in* Reise
>Nach den Aequinoctiat-Gegenden des Neuen
>Kontinents *[Voyage to the equinoctial regions of the new*
>*continent] (Book 8, Chapter 24). The warlike tribe, the*
>*Otomaco, especially use this drug, called niopo, yupa, nopo*
>*or cojoba, to an extensive degree, even today. It is reported in*
>*the monograph by P. J. Gumilla, S. J. (Et Orinoco Itustrado,*
>*1741): "The Otomacos sniffed the powder before they*
>*went to battle with the Caribes, for in earlier times there*
>*existed savage wars between these tribes... This drug robs*
>*them completely of reason, and they frantically seize their*
>*weapons. And if the women were not so adept at holding*
>*them back and binding them fast, they would daily cause*
>*horrible devastation. It is a terrible vice... Other benign and*
>*docile tribes that also sniff the yupa, do not get into such*
>*a fury as the Otomacos, who through self-injury with this*
>*agent made themselves completely cruel before combat, and*
>*marched into battle with savage fury."*

>I am curious how niopo would act on people like us.
>*Should a niopo session one day come to pass, then we should*
>*on no account send our wives away, as on that early spring*

reverie [The LSD trip of February 1951 is meant here], that
they may bind us fast if necessary...

Chemical analysis of this drug led to isolation of active
principles that, like the ergot alkaloids and psilocybin, belong to
the group of indole alkaloids, but which were already described
in the technical literature, and were therefore not investigated
further in the Sandoz laboratories. [Translator's note: The active
principles of niopo are DMT (N,N-dimethyltryptamine) and its
congeners. DMT was first prepared in 1931 by Manske.] The
fantastic effects described above appeared to occur only with the
particular manner of use as snuff powder, and also seemed to be
related, in all probability, to the psychic structure of the Indian
tribes concerned.

AMBIVALENCE ON DRUG USE

Fundamental questions of drug problems were dealt with in
the following correspondence.

Bottmingen, 16 December 1961

Dear Mr. Jünger,

On the one hand, I would have the great desire,
besides the natural-scientific, chemical-pharmacological
investigation of hallucinogenic substances, also to research
their use as magic drugs in other regions... On the other
hand, I must admit that the fundamental question very
much occupies me, whether the use of these types of drugs,
namely of substances that so deeply affect our minds, could
not indeed represent a forbidden transgression of limits. As
long as any means or methods are used, which provide only
an additional, newer aspect of reality, surely there is nothing
to object to in such means; on the contrary, the experience
and the knowledge of further facets of the reality only
makes this reality ever more real to us. The question exists,
however, whether the deeply affecting drugs under discussion
here will in fact only open an additional window for our

senses and perceptions, or whether the spectator himself,
the core of his being, undergoes alterations. The latter
would signify that something is altered that in my opinion
should always remain intact. My concern is addressed to the
question, whether the innermost core of our being is actually
unimpeachable, and cannot become damaged by whatever
happens in its material, physical-chemical, biological and
psychic shells—or whether matter in the form of these drugs
displays a potency that has the ability to attack the spiritual
center of the personality, the self. The latter would have to be
explained by the fact that the effect of magic drugs happens
at the borderline where mind and matter merge—that these
magic substances are themselves cracks in the infinite realm
of matter, in which the depth of matter, its relationship
with the mind, becomes particularly obvious. This could be
expressed by a modification of the familiar words of Goethe:

"Were the eye not sunny,
It could never behold the sun;
If the power of the mind were not in matter,
How could matter disturb the mind."

This would correspond to cracks which the radioactive
substances constitute in the periodic system of the elements,
where the transition of matter into energy becomes manifest.
Indeed, one must ask whether the production of atomic
energy likewise represents a transgression of forbidden limits.

A further disquieting thought, which follows from the
possibility of influencing the highest intellectual functions by
traces of a substance, concerns free will.

The highly active psychotropic substances like LSD
and psilocybin possess in their chemical structure a very
close relationship with substances inherent in the body,
which are found in the central nervous system and play
an important role in the regulation of its functions. It is
therefore conceivable that through some disturbance in the

metabolism of the normal neurotransmitters, a compound like LSD or psilocybin is formed that can determine and alter the character of the individual, his worldview and his behavior. A trace of a substance, whose production or nonproduction we cannot control with our wills, has the power to shape our destiny. Such biochemical considerations could have led to the sentence that Gottfried Benn quoted in his essay "Provoziertes Leben" [Provoked life]: "God is a substance, a drug!"

On the other hand, it is well known that substances like adrenaline, for example, are formed or set free in our organism by thoughts and emotions, which for their part determine the functions of the nervous system. One may therefore suppose that our material organism is susceptible to and shaped by our mind, in the same way that our intellectual essence is shaped by our biochemistry. Which came first can indeed no better be determined than the question, whether the chicken came before the egg.

In spite of my uncertainty with regard to the fundamental dangers that could lie in the use of hallucinogenic substances, I have continued investigations on the active principles of the Mexican magic morning glories, of which I wrote you briefly once before. In the seeds of this morning glory, that were called ololiuhqui by the ancient Aztecs, we found as active principles lysergic acid derivatives chemically very closely related to LSD. That was an almost unbelievable finding. I have all along had a particular love for the morning glories. They were the first flowers that I grew myself in my little child's garden. Their blue and red cups belong to the first memories of my childhood.

I recently read in a book by D. T. Suzuki, ZEN AND JAPANESE CULTURE, that the morning glory plays a great role in Japan, among the flower lovers, in literature, and

*in graphic arts. Its fleeting splendor has given the Japanese
imagination rich stimulus. Among others, Suzuki quotes
a three- line poem of the poetess Chiyo (1702-75), who
one morning went to fetch water from a neighbor's house,
because... "My trough is captivated by a morning glory
blossom, So I ask after water."*

*The morning glory thus shows both possible ways of
influencing the mind-body-essence of man: in Mexico it
exerts its effects in a chemical way as a magic drug, while in
Japan it acts from the spiritual side, through the beauty of
its flower cups.*

Wilflingen, 17 December 1961
Dear Mr. Hofmann,

*I give you my thanks for your detailed letter of 16
December. I have reflected on your central question, and
may probably become occupied with it on the occasion of the
revision of* AN DER ZEITMAUER *[At the wall of no time].
There I intimated that, in the field of physics as well as in
the field of biology, we are beginning to develop procedures
that are no longer to be understood as advances in the
established sense, but that rather intervene in evolution and
lead forth in the development of the species. Certainly I turn
the glove inside out, for I suppose that it is a new world age,
which begins to act evolutionarily on the prototypes. Our
science with its theories and discoveries is therefore not the
cause, rather one of the consequences of evolution, among
others. Animals, plants, the atmosphere and the surfaces of
planets will be concerned simultaneously. We do not progress
from point to point, rather we cross over a line.*

*The risk that you indicated is well to be considered.
However, it exists in every aspect of our existence. The
common denominator appears now here, now there.*

In mentioning radioactivity, you use the word crack.

Cracks are not merely points of discovery, but also points of destruction. Compared to the effects of radiation, those of the magical drugs are more genuine and much less rough. In classical manner they lead us beyond the humane. Gurdjieff has already seen that to some extent. Wine has already changed much, has brought new gods and a new humanity with it. But wine is to the new substances as classical physics is to modern physics. These things should only be tried in small circles. I cannot agree with the thoughts of Huxley, that possibilities for transcendence could here be given to the masses. Indeed, this does not involve comforting fictions, but rather realities, if we take the matter earnestly. And few contacts will suffice here for the setting of courses and guidance. It also transcends theology and belongs in the chapter of theogony, as it necessarily entails entry into a new house, in the astrological sense. At first, one can be satisfied with this insight, and should above all be cautious with the designations.

Heartfelt thanks also for the beautiful picture of the blue morning glory. It appears to be the same that I cultivate year after year in my garden. I did not know that it possesses specific powers; however, that is probably the case with every plant. We do not know the key to most. Besides this, there must be a central viewpoint from which not only the chemistry, the structure, the color, but rather all attributes become significant...

An Experiment with Psilocybin

Such theoretical discussions about the magic drugs were supplemented by practical experiments. One such experiment, which served as a comparison between LSD and psilocybin, took place in the spring of 1962. The proper occasion for it presented itself at the home of the Jüngers, in the former head forester's house of Stauffenberg's castle in Wilflingen. My friends, the pharmacologist Professor Heribert Konzett and the Islamic scholar Dr. Rudolf Gelpke, also took part in this mushroom symposium.

The old chronicles described how the Aztecs drank chocolatl before they ate teonanacatl. Thus Mrs. Liselotte Jünger likewide served us hot chocolate, to set the mood. Then she abandoned the four men to their fate.

We had gathered in a fashionable living room, with a dark wooden ceiling, white tile stove, period furniture, old French engravings on the walls, a gorgeous bouquet of tulips on the table. Ernst Jünger wore a long, broad, dark blue striped kaftan-like garment that he had brought from Egypt; Heribert Konzett was resplendent in a brightly embroidered mandarin gown; Rudolf Gelpke and I had put on housecoats. The everyday reality should be laid aside, along with everyday clothing.

Shortly before sundown we took the drug, not the mushrooms, but rather their active principle, 20 mg psilocybin each. That corresponded to some two-thirds of the very strong dose that was taken by the curandera Maria Sabina in the form of *Psilocybe* mushrooms.

After an hour I still noticed no effect, while my companions were already very deeply into the trip. I had come with the hope that in the mushroom inebriation I could manage to allow certain images from euphoric moments of my childhood, which remained in my memory as blissful experiences, to come alive: a meadow covered with chrysanthemums lightly stirred by the early summer wind; the rosebush in the evening light after a rain storm; the blue irises hanging over the vineyard wall. Instead of these bright images from my childhood home, strange scenery emerged, when the mushroom factor finally began to act. Half stupefied, I sank deeper, passed through totally deserted cities with a Mexican type of exotic, yet dead splendor. Terrified, I tried to detain myself on the surface, to concentrate alertly on the outer world, on the surroundings. For a time I succeeded. I then observed Ernst Jünger, colossal in the room, pacing back and forth, a powerful, mighty magician. Heribert Konzett in the silky lustrous housecoat seemed to be a dangerous, Chinese clown. Even Rudolf Gelpke appeared sinister to me; long, thin, mysterious.

With the increasing depth of inebriation, everything became yet stranger. I even felt strange to myself. Weird, cold, foolish, deserted, in a dull light, were the places I traversed when I closed my eyes. Emptied of all meaning, the environment also seemed ghostlike to me whenever I opened my eyes and tried to cling to the outer world. The total emptiness threatened to drag me down into absolute nothingness. I remember how I seized Rudolf Gelpke's arm as he passed by my chair, and held myself to him, in order not to sink into dark nothingness. Fear of death seized me, and illimitable longing to return to the living creation, to the reality of the world of men. After timeless fear I slowly returned to the room . I saw and heard the great magician lecturing uninterruptedly with a clear, loud voice, about Schopenhauer, Kant, Hegel, and speaking about the old Gaia, the beloved little mother. Heribert Konzett and Rudolf Gelpke were already completely on the earth again, while I could only regain my footing with great effort.

For me this entry into the mushroom world had been a test, a confrontation with a dead world and with the void. The experiment had developed differently from what I had expected. Nevertheless, the encounter with the void can also be appraised as a gain. Then the existence of the creation appears so much more wondrous.

Midnight had passed, as we sat together at the table that the mistress of the house had set in the upper story. We celebrated the return with an exquisite repast and with Mozart's music. The conversation, during which we exchanged our experiences, lasted almost until morning.

Ernst Jünger has described how he had experienced this trip, in his book *Annahenngenrogen und Rausch* [Approaches: drugs and inebriation] (published by Ernst Klett Verlag, Stuttgart, 1970), in the section *"Ein Pilz-Symposium"* [A mushroom symposium]. The following is an extract from the work:

As usual, a half hour or a little more passed in silence. Then came the first signs: the flowers on the table began to flare up and sent out flashes. It was time for leaving work; outside the streets were being cleaned, like on every weekend. The brushstrokes invaded the silence painfully. This shuffling and brushing, now and again also a scraping, pounding, rumbling, and hammering, has random causes and is also symptomatic, like one of the signs that announces an illness. Again and again it also plays a role in the history of magic practices.

By this time the mushroom began to act; the spring bouquet glowed darker. That was no natural light. The shadows stirred in the corners, as if they sought form. I became uneasy, even chilled, despite the heat that emanated from the tiles. I stretched myself on the sofa, drew the covers over my head.

Everything became skin and was touched, even the retina—there the contact was light. This light was multicolored, it arranged itself in strings, which gently swung back and forth; in strings of glass beads of Oriental doorways. They formed doors, like those one passes through in a dream, curtains of lust and danger. The wind stirred them like a garment. They also fell down from the belts of dancers, opened and closed themselves with the swing of the hips, and from the beads a rippling of the most delicate sounds fluttered to the heightened senses. The chime of the silver rings on the ankles and wrists is already too loud. It smells of sweat, blood, tobacco, chopped horse hairs, cheap rose essence. Who knows what is going on in the stables?

It must be an immense palace, Mauritanian, not a good place. At this ballroom flights of adjoining rooms lead into the lower stratum. And everywhere the curtains with their

*glitter, their sparkling, radioactive glow. Moreover, the
rippling of glassy instruments with their beckoning, their
wooing solicitation: "Will you go with me, beautiful boy?"
Now it ceased, now it repeated, more importunate, more
intrusive, almost already assured of agreement.*

*Now came forms—historical collages, the vox humana,
the call of the cuckoo. Was it the whore of Santa Lucia, who
stuck her breasts out of the window? Then the play was
ruined. Salome danced; the amber necklace emitted sparks
and made the nipples erect. What would one not do for one's
Johannes? [Translator's note: "Johannes" here is slang for
penis, as in English "Dick" or "Peter."] Damned, that was a
disgusting obscenity, which did not come from me, but was
whispered through the curtain.*

*The snakes were dirty, scarcely alive, they wallowed
sluggishly over the floor mats. They were garnished with
brilliant shards. Others looked up from the floor with red
and green eyes. It glistened and whispered, hissed and
sparkled like diminutive sickles at the sacred harvest. Then
it quieted, and came anew, more faintly, more forward. They
had me in their hand. "There we immediately understood
ourselves."*

*Madam came through the curtain: she was busy, passed
by me without noticing me. I saw the boots with the red
heels. Garters constricted the thick thighs in the middle,
the flesh bulged out there. The enormous breasts, the dark
delta of the Amazon, parrots, piranhas, semiprecious stones
everywhere. Now she went into the kitchen—or are there
still cellars here? The sparkling and whispering, the hissing
and twinkling could no longer be differentiated; it seemed to
become concentrated, now proudly rejoicing, full of hope.*

*It became hot and intolerable; I threw the covers off. The
room was faintly illuminated; the pharmacologist stood at
the window in the white mandarin frock, which had served*

me shortly before in Rottweil at the carnival. The Orientalist sat beside the tile stove; he moaned as if he had a nightmare. I understood; it had been a first round, and it would soon start again. The time was not yet up. I had already seen the beloved little mother under other circumstances. But even excrement is earth, belongs like gold to transformed matter. One must come to terms with it, without getting too close.

These were the earthy mushrooms. More light was hidden in the dark grain that burst from the ear, more yet in the green juice of the succulents on the glowing slopes of Mexico.... [Translator's note: Jünger is referring to LSD, a derivative of ergot, and mescaline, derived from the Mexican peyotl cactus.]

The trip had run awry—possibly I should address the mushrooms once more. Yet indeed the whispering returned, the flashing and sparkling—the bait pulled the fish close behind itself. Once the motif is given, then it engraves itself, like on a roller each new beginning, each new revolution repeats the melody. The game did not get beyond this kind of dreariness.

I don't know how often this was repeated, and prefer not to dwell upon it. Also, there are things which one would rather keep to oneself. In any case, midnight was past...

We went upstairs; the table was set. The senses were still heightened and the Doors of Perception were opened. The light undulated from the red wine in the carafe; a froth surged at the brim. We listened to a flute concerto. It had not turned out better for the others: "How beautiful, to be back among men." Thus Albert Hofmann.

The Orientalist on the other hand had been in Samarkand, where Timur rests in a coffin of nephrite. He had followed the victorious march through cities, whose dowry on entry was a cauldron filled with eyes. There he had long stood before one of the skull pyramids that terrible

*Timur had erected, and in the multitude of severed heads had
perceived even his own. It was encrusted with stones.*

*A light dawned on the pharmacologist when he heard
this: "Now I know why you were sitting in the armchair
without your head"—I was astonished; I knew I wasn't
dreaming.*

*I wonder whether I should not strike out this detail since
it borders on the area of ghost stories.*

The mushroom substance had carried all four of us off, not
into luminous heights, rather into deeper regions. It seems that
the psilocybin inebriation is more darkly colored in the majority
of cases than the inebriation produced by LSD. The influence of
these two active substances is sure to differ from one individual
to another. Personally, for me, there was more light in the LSD
experiments than in the experiments with the earthy mushroom,
just as Ernst Jünger remarks in the preceding report.

ANOTHER LSD SESSION

The next and last thrust into the inner universe together with
Ernst Jünger, this time again using LSD, led us very far from
everyday consciousness. We came close to the ultimate door. Of
course this door, according to Ernst Jünger, will in fact only open
for us in the great transition from life into the hereafter.

This last joint experiment occurred in February 1970, again at
the head forester's house in Wilflingen. In this case there were
only the two of us. Ernst Jünger took 0.15 mg LSD, I took 0.10 mg.
Ernst Jünger has published without commentary the log book,
the notes he made during the experiment, in *Approaches*, in the
section "Nochmals LSD" [LSD once again]. They are scanty and
tell the reader little, just like my own records.

The experiment lasted from morning just after breakfast until
darkness fell. At the beginning of the trip, we again listened to
the concerto for flute and harp by Mozart, which always made
me especially happy, but this time, strange to say, seemed to me

like the turning of porcelain figures. Then the intoxication led quickly into wordless depths. When I wanted to describe the perplexing alterations of consciousness to Ernst Jünger, no more than two or three words came out, for they sounded so false, so unable to express the experience; they seemed to originate from an infinitely distant world that had become strange; I abandoned the attempt, laughing hopelessly. Obviously, Ernst Jünger had the same experience, yet we did not need speech; a glance sufficed for the deepest understanding. I could, however, put some scraps of sentences on paper, such as at the beginning: "Our boat tosses violently." Later, upon regarding expensively bound books in the library: "Like red-gold pushed from within to without—exuding golden luster." Outside it began to snow. Masked children marched past and carts with carnival revelers passed by in the streets. With a glance through the window into the garden, in which snow patches lay, many-colored masks appeared over the high walls bordering it, embedded in an infinitely joyful shade of blue: "A Breughel garden—I live with and in the objects." Later: "At present no connection with the everyday world." Toward the end, deep, comforting insight expressed: "Until now confirmed on my path." This time LSD had led to a delightful encounter.

Chapter 8
Meeting with Aldous Huxley

IN THE MID-1950S, two books by Aldous Huxley appeared,
The Doors of Perception and *Heaven and Hell*, dealing with
inebriated states produced by hallucinogenic drugs. The
alterations of sensory perceptions and consciousness, which
the author experienced in a self-experiment with mescaline, are
skillfully described in these books. The mescaline experiment was
a visionary experience for Huxley. He saw objects in a new light;
they disclosed their inherent, deep, timeless existence, which
remains hidden from everyday sight.

These two books contained fundamental observations on the
essence of visionary experience and about the significance of this
manner of comprehending the world—in cultural history, in the
creation of myths, in the origin of religions, and in the creative
process out of which works of art arise. Huxley saw the value of
hallucinogenic drugs in that they give people who lack the gift of
spontaneous visionary perception, belonging to mystics, saints,
and great artists, the potential to experience this extraordinary
state of consciousness, and thereby to attain insight into the
spiritual world of these great creators. Hallucinogens could lead
to a deepened understanding of religious and mystical content,
and to a new and fresh experience of the great works of art. For
Huxley these drugs were keys capable of opening new doors
of perception; chemical keys, in addition to other proven but
laborious " door openers" to the visionary world, like meditation,
isolation, and fasting, or like certain yoga practices.

At the time I already knew the earlier work of this great writer and thinker, books that meant much to me, like *Point Counter Point, Brave New World, After Many a Summer, Eyeless in Gaza*, and a few others. In *The Doors of Perception* and *Heaven and Hell*, Huxley's newly-published works, I found a meaningful exposition of the experience induced by hallucinogenic drugs, and I thereby gained a deepened insight into my own LSD experiments.

I was therefore delighted when I received a telephone call from Aldous Huxley in the laboratory one morning in August 1961. He was passing through Zurich with his wife. He invited me and my wife to lunch in the Hotel Sonnenberg.

A gentleman with a yellow freesia in his buttonhole, a tall and noble appearance, who exuded kindness—this is the image I retained from this first meeting with Aldous Huxley. The table conversation revolved mainly around the problem of magic drugs. Both Huxley and his wife, Laura Archera Huxley, had also experimented with LSD and psilocybin. Huxley would have preferred not to designate these two substances and mescaline as "drugs," because in English usage, as also, by the way, with *Droge* in German, that word has a pejorative connotation, and because it was important to differentiate the hallucinogens from the other drugs, even linguistically. He believed in the great importance of agents producing visionary experience in the modern phase of human evolution.

He considered experiments under laboratory conditions to be insignificant, since in the extraordinarily intensified susceptibility and sensitivity to external impressions, the surroundings are of decisive importance. He recommended to my wife, when we spoke of her native place in the mountains, that she take LSD in an alpine meadow and then look into the blue cup of a gentian flower, to behold the wonder of creation.

As we parted, Aldous Huxley gave me, as a remembrance of this meeting, a tape recording of his lecture "Visionary Experience," which he had delivered the week before at an international congress on applied psychology in Copenhagen. In

this lecture, Aldous Huxley spoke about the meaning and essence
of visionary experience and compared this type of worldview
to the verbal and intellectual comprehension of reality as its
essential complement.

In the following year, the newest and last book by Aldous
Huxley appeared, the novel *Island*. This story, set on the utopian
island Pala, is an attempt to blend the achievements of natural
science and technical civilization with the wisdom of Eastern
thought, to achieve a new culture in which rationalism and
mysticism are fruitfully united. The *moksha* medicine, a magical
drug prepared from a mushroom, plays a significant role in the
life of the population of Pala (moksha is Sanskrit for "release,"
"liberation"). The drug could be used only in critical periods of
life. The young people on Pala received it in initiation rites, it
is dispensed to the protagonist of the novel during a life crisis,
in the scope of a psychotherapeutic dialogue with a spiritual
friend, and it helps the dying to relinquish the mortal body, in the
transition to another existence.

In our conversation in Zurich, I had already learned from
Aldous Huxley that he would again treat the problem of
psychedelic drugs in his forthcoming novel. Now he sent me a
copy of *Island*, inscribed "To Dr. Albert Hofmann the original
discoverer of the moksha medicine, from Aldous Huxley."

The hopes that Aldous Huxley placed in psychedelic drugs as
a means of evoking visionary experience, and the uses of these
substances in everyday life, are subjects of a letter of 29 February
1962, in which he wrote me:

> ...I have good hopes that this and similar work will result
> in the development of a real Natural History of visionary
> experience, in all its variations, determined by differences of
> physique, temperament and profession, and at the same time
> of a technique of Applied Mysticism—a technique for helping
> individuals to get the most out of their transcendental
> experience and to make use of the insights from the "OTHER

WORLD" *in the affairs of "This World." Meister Eckhart*
wrote that "what is taken in by contemplation must be given
out in love." Essentially this is what must be developed—the
art of giving out in love and intelligence what is taken in
from vision and the experience of self-transcendence and
solidarity with the Universe...

Aldous Huxley and I were together often at the annual
convention of the World Academy of Arts and Sciences (WAAS)
in Stockholm during late summer 1963. His suggestions and
contributions to discussions at the sessions of the academy,
through their form and importance, had a great influence on the
proceedings.

WAAS had been established in order to allow the most
competent specialists to consider world problems in a forum free
of ideological and religious restrictions and from an international
viewpoint encompassing the whole world. The results: proposals,
and thoughts in the form of appropriate publications, were to
be placed at the disposal of the responsible governments and
executive organizations.

The 1963 meeting of WAAS had dealt with the population
explosion and the raw material reserves and food resources
of the earth. The corresponding studies and proposals were
collected in Volume II of WAAS under the title *The Population
Crisis and the Use of World Resources.* A decade before birth
control, environmental protection, and the energy crisis became
catchwords, these world problems were examined there from
the most serious point of view, and proposals for their solution
were made to governments and responsible organizations. The
catastrophic events since that time in the aforementioned fields
makes evident the tragic discrepancy between recognition, desire,
and feasibility.

Aldous Huxley made the proposal, as a continuation and
complement of the theme "World Resources" at the Stockholm
convention, to address the problem "Human Resources," the

exploration and application of capabilities hidden in humans yet unused. A human race with more highly developed spiritual capacities, with expanded consciousness of the depth and the incomprehensible wonder of being, would also have greater understanding of and better consideration for the biological and material foundations of life on this earth. Above all, for Western people with their hypertrophied rationality, the development and expansion of a direct, emotional experience of reality, unobstructed by words and concepts, would be of evolutionary significance. Huxley considered psychedelic drugs to be one means to achieve education in this direction. The psychiatrist Dr. Humphry Osmond likewise participating in the congress, who had created the term psychedelic (mind-expanding), assisted him with a report about significant possibilities of the use of hallucinogens.

The convention in Stockholm in 1963 was my last meeting with Aldous Huxley. His physical appearance was already marked by a severe illness; his intellectual personage, however, still bore the undiminished signs of a comprehensive knowledge of the heights and depths of the inner and outer world of man, which he had displayed with so much genius, love, goodness, and humor in his literary work.

Aldous Huxley died on 22 November of the same year, on the same day President Kennedy was assassinated. From Laura Huxley I obtained a copy of her letter to Julian and Juliette Huxley, in which she reported to her brother- and sister-in-law about her husband's last day. The doctors had prepared her for a dramatic end, because the terminal phase of cancer of the throat, from which Aldous Huxley suffered, is usually accompanied by convulsions and choking fits. He died serenely and peacefully, however.

In the morning, when he was already so weak that he could no longer speak, he had written on a sheet of paper: "LSD—try it—intramuscular—100 mcg." Mrs. Huxley understood what was meant by this, and ignoring the misgivings of the attending physician, she gave him, with her own hand, the desired injection—she let him have the moksha medicine.

Chapter 9
Correspondence with the Poet-Physician Walter Vogt

MY FRIENDSHIP WITH THE PHYSICIAN, psychiatrist, and writer
Walter Vogt, M.D., is also among the personal contacts that I
owe to LSD. As the following extract from our correspondence
shows, it was less the medicinal aspects of LSD, important to the
physician, than the consciousness-altering effects on the depth of
the psyche, of interest to the writer, that constituted the theme of
our correspondence.

Muri/Bern, 22 November 1970

Dear Mr. Hofmann,

*Last night I dreamed that I was invited to tea in a cafe by
a friendly family in Rome. This family also knew the pope,
and so the pope sat at the same table to tea with us. He was
all in white and also wore a white miter. He sat there so
handsome and was silent.*

*And today I suddenly had the idea of sending you
my* VOGEL AUF DEM TISCH *[Bird on the table] —as a
visiting card if you so wish—a book that remained a little
apocryphal, which upon reflection I do not regret, although
the Italian translator is firmly convinced that is my best.
(Ah yes, the pope is also an Italian. So it goes...)*

*Possibly this little work will interest you. It was written
in 1966 by an author who at that time still had not had any
shred of experience with psychedelic substances and who read
the reports about medicinal experiments with these drugs
devoid of understanding. However, little has changed since,
except that now the misgiving comes from the other side.*

I suppose that your discovery has caused a hiatus (not directly a Saul-to-Paul conversion as Roland Fischer says...) in my work (also a large word)—and indeed, that which I have written since has become rather realistic or at least less expressive. In any case I could not have brought off the cool realism of my TV piece "SPIELE DER MACHT" [Games of Power] without it. The different drafts attest it, in case they are still lying around somewhere.

Should you have interest and time for a meeting, it would delight me very much to visit you sometime for a conversation. Burg, i.L. 28 November 1970

Dear Mr. Vogt,

If the bird that alighted on my table was able to find its way to me, this is one more debt I owe to the magical effect of LSD. I could soon write a book about all of the results that derive from that experiment in 1943...

A. H.

Muri/Bern, 13 March 1971

Mr. Hofmann,

Enclosed is a critique of Jünger's ANNAHENNGEN [Approaches], from the daily paper, that will presumably interest you...

It seems to me that to hallucinate—to dream—to write—stands at all times in contrast to everyday consciousness, and their functions are complementary. Here I can naturally speak only for myself. This could be different with others – it is also truly difficult to speak with others about such things, because people often speak altogether different languages...

However, since you are now gathering autographs, and do me the honor of incorporating some of my letters in your collection, I enclose for you the manuscript of my "testament"—in which your discovery plays a role as "the

only joyous invention of the twentieth century..."
W. V.

*dr. walter vogts most recent testament 1969 I wish to
have no special funeral only expensive and obscene orchids
innumerable little birds with gay names no naked dancers
but psychedelic garments loudspeaker in every corner and
nothing but the latest beatles record* [ABBEY ROAD] *one
hundred thousand million times and do what you like
["Blind Faith"] on an endless tape nothing more than a
popular Christ with a halo of genuine gold and a beloved
mourning congregation that pumped themselves full with
acid [acid = LSD] till they go to heaven [From* ABBEY
ROAD, *side two] one two three four five six seven possibly we
will encounter one another there most cordially dedicated to
Dr. Albert Hofmann*

Beginning of Spring 1971
Burg i.L., 29 March 1971
Dear Mr. Vogt,
*You have again presented me with a lovely letter and a
very valuable autograph, the testament 1969...*
*Very remarkable dreams in recent times induce me to
test a connection between the composition (chemical) of the
evening meal and the quality of dreams. Yes, LSD is also
something that one eats...*
A. H.

Muri/Bern, 5 September 1971
Mr. Hofmann,
*Over the weekend at Murtensee [On that Sunday, I
(A. H.) hovered over the Murtensee in the balloon of my
friend E. I., who had taken me along as passenger.], I often
thought of you—a most radiant autumn day. Yesterday,*

*Saturday, thanks to one tablet of aspirin (on account
of a headache or mild flu), I experienced a very comical
flashback, like with mescaline (of which I have had only a
little, exactly once)...*

*I have read a delightful essay by Wasson about
mushrooms; he divides mankind into mycophobes and
mycophiles... Lovely fly agarics must now be growing in the
forest near you. Sometime shouldn't we sample some?*

W. V.

Muri/Bern, 7 September 1971
Mr. Hofmann,

*Now I feel I must write briefly to tell you what I have
done outside in the sun, on the dock under your balloon:
I finally wrote some notes about our visit in Villars-sur-
Ollons (with Dr. Leary), then a hippie-bark went by on the
lake, self-made like from a Fellini film, which I sketched, and
over and above it I drew your balloon.*

W. V.

Burg i.L., 15 April 1972
Dear Mr. Vogt,

*Your television play "SPIELE DER MACHT" [Games of
power] has impressed me extraordinarily.*

*I congratulate you on this magnificent piece, which
allows mental cruelty to become conscious, and therefore
also acts in its way as "consciousness-expanding," and
can thereby prove itself therapeutic in a higher sense, like
ancient tragedy.*

A. H.

Burg i.L., 19 May 1973
Dear Mr. Vogt,

Now I have already read your lay sermon three times,

*the description and interpretation of your Sinai Trip. [Walter
Vogt: "Mein Sinai Trip. Eine Laienpredigt" [My Sinai trip: A lay sermon]
(Verlag der Arche, Zurich, 1972). This publication contains the text of a
lay sermon that Walter Vogt gave on 14 November 1971 on the invitation
of Parson Christoph Mohl, in the Protestant church of aduz (Lichtenstein),
in the course of a series of sermons by writers, and in addition contains
an afterword by the author and by the inviting parson. It involves the
description and interpretation of an ecstatic-religious experience evoked by
LSD, that the author is able to "place in a distant, if you will superficial,
analogy to the great Sinai Trip of Moses." It is not only the "patriarchal
atmosphere" that is to be traced out of these descriptions that constitutes
this analogy; there are deeper references, which are more to be read between
the lines of this text.]*

Was it really an LSD trip?... It was a courageous deed,
to choose such a notorious event as a drug experience as the
theme of a sermon, even a lay sermon. But the questions
raised by hallucinogenic drugs do actually belong in the
church—in a prominent place in the church, for they are
sacred drugs (peyotl, teonanacatl, ololiuhqui, with which
LSD is mostly closely related by chemical structure and
activity).

I can fully agree with what you say in your introduction
about the modern ecclesiastical religiosity: the three
sanctioned states of consciousness (the waking condition
of uninterrupted work and performance of duty, alcoholic
intoxication, and sleep), the distinction between two phases
of psychedelic inebriation (the first phase, the peak of the
trip, in which the cosmic relationship is experienced, or the
submersion into one's own body, in which everything that is,
is within; and the second phase, characterized as the phase
of enhanced comprehension of symbols), and the allusion to
the candor that hallucinogens bring about in consciousness
states. These are all observations that are of fundamental
importance in the judgement of hallucinogenic inebriation.

*The most worthwhile spiritual benefit from LSD experiments
was the experience of the inextricable intertwining of the
physical and spiritual. "Christ in matter" (Teilhard de
Chardin). Did the insight first come to you also through
your drug experiences, that we must descend "into the flesh,
which we are," in order to get new prophesies?*

*A criticism of your sermon: you allow the "deepest
experience that there is"—"The kingdom of heaven is within
you"—to be uttered by Timothy Leary. This sentence,
quoted without the indication of its true source, could be
interpreted as ignorance of one—or rather the principal—
truth of Christian belief.*

*One of your statements deserves universal recognition:
"There is no non-ecstatic religious experience."...*

*Next Monday evening I shall be interviewed on Swiss
television (about LSD and the Mexican magic drugs, on the
program "AT FIRST HAND"). I am curious about the sort of
questions that will be asked...*

A. H.

Muri/Bern, 24 May 1973
Dear Mr. Hofmann,

*Of course it was LSD—only I did not want to write
about it explicitly, I really do not know just why myself...
The great emphasis I placed on the good Leary, who now
seems to me to be somewhat flipped out, as the prime
witness, can indeed only be explained by the special context
of the talk or sermon.*

*I must admit that the perception that we must descend
"into the flesh, which we are" actually first came to me with
LSD. I still ruminate on it, possibly it even came "too late"
for me in fact, although more and more I advocate your
opinion that LSD should be taboo for youth (taboo, not*

forbidden, that is the difference...

The sentence that you like, "there is no nonecstatic religious experience," was apparently not liked so much by others for example, by my (almost only) literary friend and minister-lyric poet Kurt Marti... But in any case, we are practically never of the same opinion about anything, and notwithstanding, we constitute, when we occasionally communicate by phone and arrange little activities together, the smallest minimafia of Switzerland.

W. V.

Burg i.L., 13 April 1974

Dear Mr. Vogt,

Full of suspense, we watched your TV play "PILATE BEFORE THE SILENT CHRIST" yesterday evening.

...as a representation of the fundamental man-God relationship: man, who comes to God with his most difficult questions, which finally he must answer himself, because God is silent. He does not answer them with words. The answers are contained in the book of his creation (to which the questioning man himself belongs). True natural science deciphering of this text.

A. H.

Muri/Bern, 11 May 1974

Dear Mr. Hofmann,

I have composed a "poem" in half twilight, that I dare to send to you. At first I wanted to send it to Leary, but this would make no sense.

Leary in jail. Gelpke is dead. Treatment in the asylum... is this your psychedelic revolution? Had we taken seriously something with which one only ought to play or vice-versa...

W. V.

Chapter 10
Various Visitors

THE DIVERSE ASPECTS, the multi-faceted emanations of LSD
are also expressed in the variety of cultural circles with which
this substance has brought me into contact. On the scientific
plane, this has involved colleagues—chemists, pharmacologists,
physicians, and mycologists—whom I met at universities,
congresses, lectures, or with whom I came into association
through publication. In the literary-philosophical field there were
contacts with writers. In the preceding chapters I have reported
on the relationships of this type that were most significant for
me. LSD also provided me with a variegated series of personal
acquaintances from the drug scene and from hippie circles, which
will briefly be described here.

Most of these visitors came from the United States and were
young people, often in transit to the Far East in search of Eastern
wisdom or of a guru; or else hoping to come by drugs more easily
there. Prague also was sometimes the goal, because LSD of good
quality could at the time easily be acquired there. [Translator's
Note: When Sandoz's patents on LSD expired in 1963, the Czech
pharmaceutical firm Spofa began to manufacture the drug.]
Once arrived in Europe, they wanted to take advantage of the
opportunity to see the father of LSD, "the man who made the
famous LSD bicycle trip." But more serious concerns sometimes
motivated a visit. There was the desire to report on personal LSD
experiences and to debate the purport of their meaning, at the
source, so to speak. Only rarely did a visit prove to be inspired
by the desire to obtain LSD, when a visitor hinted that he or she

wished to once experiment with most assuredly pure material, with original LSD.

Visitors of various types and with diverse desires also came from Switzerland and other European countries. Such encounters have become rarer in recent times, which may be related to the fact that LSD has become less important in the drug scene. Whenever possible, I have welcomed such visitors or agreed to meet somewhere. This I considered to be an obligation connected with my role in the history of LSD, and I have tried to help by instructing and advising.

Sometimes no true conversation occurred, for example with the inhibited young man who arrived on a motorbike. I was not clear about the objective of his visit. He stared at me, as if asking himself: can the man who has made something so weird as LSD really look so completely ordinary? With him, as with other similar visitors, I had the feeling that he hoped, in my presence, the LSD riddle would somehow solve itself.

Other meetings were completely different, like the one with the young man from Toronto. He invited me to lunch at an exclusive restaurant—impressive appearance, tall, slender, a businessman, proprietor of an important industrial firm in Canada, brilliant intellect. He thanked me for the creation of LSD, which had given his life another direction. He had been 100 percent a businessman, with a purely materialistic worldview. LSD had opened his eyes to the spiritual aspect of life. Now he possessed a sense for art, literature, and philosophy and was deeply concerned with religious and metaphysical questions. He now desired to make the LSD experience accessible in a suitable milieu to his young wife, and hoped for a similarly fortunate transformation in her.

Not as profound, yet still liberating and rewarding, were the results of LSD experiments which a young Dane described to me with much humor and fantasy. He came from California, where he had been a houseboy for Henry Miller in Big Sur. He moved on to France with the plan of acquiring a dilapidated farm there, which he, a skilled carpenter, then wanted to restore himself. I asked him to obtain an autograph of his former employer for my collection, and after some time I actually received an original piece of writing from Henry Miller's hand.

A young woman sought me out to report on LSD experiences that had been of great significance to her inner development. As a superficial teenager who pursued all sorts of entertainments, and quite neglected by her parents, she had begun to take LSD out of curiosity and love of adventure. For three years she took frequent LSD trips. They led to an astonishing intensification of her inner life. She began to seek after the deeper meaning of her existence, which eventually revealed itself to her. Then, recognizing that LSD had no further power to help her, without difficulty or exertion of will she was able to abandon the drug. Thereafter she was in a position to develop herself further without artificial means. She was now a happy, intrinsically secure person—thus she concluded her report. This young woman had decided to tell me her history because she supposed that I was often attacked by narrow minded persons who saw only the damage that LSD sometimes caused among youths. The immediate motive of her testimony was a conversation that she had accidentally overheard on a railway journey. A man complained about me, finding it disgraceful that I had spoken on the LSD problem in an interview published in the newspaper. In his opinion, I ought to denounce LSD as primarily the devil's work and should publicly admit my guilt in the matter.

Persons in LSD delirium, whose condition could have given rise to such indignant condemnation, have never personally come into my sight. Such cases, attributable to LSD consumption under irresponsible circumstances, to overdosage, or to psychotic predisposition, always landed in the hospital or at the police station. Great publicity always came their way.

A visit by one young American girl stands out in my memory

as an example of the tragic effects of LSD. It was during the lunch hour, which I normally spent in my office under strict confinement—no visitors, secretary's office closed up. Knocking came at the door, discretely but firmly repeated, until eventually I went to open it. I scarcely believed my eyes: before me stood a very beautiful young woman, blond, with large blue eyes, wearing a long hippie dress, headband, and sandals. "I am Joan, I come from New York—you are Dr. Hofmann?" Before I inquired what brought her to me, I asked her how she had got through the two checkpoints, at the main entrance to the factory area and at the door of the laboratory building, for visitors were admitted only after telephone query, and this flower child must have been especially noticeable. "I am an angel, I can pass everywhere," she replied. Then she explained that she came on a great mission. She had to rescue her country, the United States; above all she had to direct the president (at the time L. B. Johnson) onto the correct path. This could be accomplished only by having him take LSD. Then he would receive the good ideas that would enable him to lead the country out of war and internal difficulties.

Joan had come to me hoping that I would help her fulfill her mission, namely to give LSD to the president. Her name would indicate she was the Joan of Arc of the USA. I don't know whether my arguments, advanced with all consideration of her holy zeal, were able to convince her that her plan had no prospects of success on psychological, technical, internal, and external grounds. Disappointed and sad she went away. Next day I received a telephone call from Joan. She again asked me to help her, since her financial resources were exhausted. I took her to a friend in Zurich who provided her with work, and with whom she could live. Joan was a teacher by profession, and also a nightclub pianist and singer. For a while she played and sang in a fashionable Zurich restaurant. The good bourgeois clients of course had no idea what sort of angel sat at the grand piano in a black evening dress and entertained them with sensitive playing and a soft and sensuous voice. Few paid attention to the words of her songs; they were for the most part hippie songs, many of them containing veiled praise of drugs. The Zurich performance did not last long; within a few weeks I learned from my friend that Joan had suddenly disappeared. He received a greeting card from her three months later, from Israel. She had been committed to a psychiatric hospital there.

For the conclusion of my assortment of LSD visitors, I wish to report about a meeting in which LSD figured only indirectly. Miss H. S., head secretary in a hospital, wrote to ask me for a personal interview. She came to tea. She explained her visit thus: in a report about an LSD experience, she had read the description of a condition she herself had experienced as a young girl, which still disturbed her today; possibly I could help her to understand this experience.

She had gone on a business trip as a commercial apprentice. They spent the night in a mountain hotel. H. S. awoke very early and left the house alone in order to watch the sunrise. As the mountains began to light up in a sea of rays, she was perfused by an unprecedented feeling of happiness, which persisted even after she joined the other participants of the trip at morning service in the chapel. During the Mass everything appeared to her in a supernatural luster, and the feeling of happiness intensified to such an extent that she had to cry loudly. She was brought back to the hotel and treated as someone with a mental disorder.

This experience largely determined her later personal life. H.S. feared she was not completely normal. On the one hand, she feared this experience, which had been explained to her as a nervous breakdown; on the other hand, she longed for a repetition of the condition. Internally split, she had led an unstable life. In repeated vocational changes and in varying personal relationships, consciously or unconsciously, she again sought this ecstatic outlook, which once made her so deeply happy.

I was able to reassure my visitor. It was no psychopathological event, no nervous breakdown that she had experienced at the time. What many people seek to attain with the help of LSD, the visionary experience of a deeper reality, had come to her as spontaneous grace. I recommended a book by Aldous Huxley to her, *The Perennial Philosophy* (Harper, New York & London, 1945) a collection of reports of spontaneous blessed visions from all times and cultures. Huxley wrote that not only mystics and saints, but also many more ordinary people than one generally supposes, experience such blessed moments, but that most do not recognize their importance and, instead of regarding them as promising rays of hope, repress them, because they do not fit into everyday rationality.

Chapter 11
LSD Experience and Reality

Was kann ein Mensch im Leben mehr gewinnen
Als dass sich Gott-Natur ihm offenbare?
What more can a person gain in life
Than that God-Nature reveals Himself to him?
– Goethe

I AM OFTEN ASKED what has made the deepest impression upon me in my LSD experiments, and whether I have arrived at new understandings through these experiences.

VARIOUS REALITIES

Of greatest significance to me has been the insight that I attained as a fundamental understanding from all of my LSD experiments: what one commonly takes as "the reality," including the reality of one's own individual person, by no means signifies something fixed, but rather something that is ambiguous—that there is not only one, but that there are many realities, each comprising also a different consciousness of the ego.

One can also arrive at this insight through scientific reflections. The problem of reality is and has been from time immemorial a central concern of philosophy. It is, however, a fundamental distinction, whether one approaches the problem of reality rationally, with the logical methods of philosophy, or if one obtrudes upon this problem emotionally, through an existential experience. The first planned LSD experiment was therefore so deeply moving and alarming, because everyday reality and the ego experiencing it, which I had until then considered to be the only reality, dissolved, and an unfamiliar ego experienced another, unfamiliar reality. The problem concerning the innermost self also appeared, which, itself unmoved, was able to record these external and internal transformations.

Reality is inconceivable without an experiencing subject, without an ego. It is the product of the exterior world, of the sender and of a receiver, an ego in whose deepest self the emanations of the exterior world, registered by the antennae of the sense organs, become conscious. If one of the two is lacking, no reality happens, no radio music plays, the picture screen remains blank.

If one continues with the conception of reality as a product of sender and receiver, then the entry of another reality under the influence of LSD may be explained by the fact that the brain, the seat of the receiver, becomes biochemically altered. The receiver is thereby tuned into another wavelength than that corresponding to normal, everyday reality. Since the endless variety and diversity of the universe correspond to infinitely many different wavelengths, depending on the adjustment of the receiver, many different realities, including the respective ego, can become conscious. These different realities, more correctly designated as different aspects of *the* reality, are not mutually exclusive but are complementary, and form together a portion of the all-encompassing, timeless, transcendental reality, in which even the unimpeachable core of self-consciousness, which has the power to record the different egos, is located.

The true importance of LSD and related hallucinogens lies in their capacity to shift the wavelength setting of the receiving "self," and thereby to evoke alterations in reality consciousness. This ability to allow different, new pictures of reality to arise, this truly cosmogonic power, makes the cultish worship of hallucinogenic plants as sacred drugs understandable.

What constitutes the essential, characteristic difference

between everyday reality and the world picture experienced
in LSD inebriation? Ego and the outer world are separated in
the normal condition of consciousness, in everyday reality; one
stands face-to-face with the outer world; it has become an object.
In the LSD state the boundaries between the experiencing self
and the outer world more or less disappear, depending on the
depth of the inebriation. Feedback between receiver and sender
takes place. A portion of the self overflows into the outer world,
into objects, which begin to live, to have another, a deeper
meaning. This can be perceived as a blessed, or as a demonic
transformation imbued with terror, proceeding to a loss of the
trusted ego. In an auspicious case, the new ego feels blissfully
united with the objects of the outer world and consequently also
with its fellow beings. This experience of deep oneness with the
exterior world can even intensify to a feeling of the self being
one with the universe. This condition of cosmic consciousness,
which under favorable conditions can be evoked by LSD or by
another hallucinogen from the group of Mexican sacred drugs,
is analogous to spontaneous religious enlightenment, with the
unio mystica. In both conditions, which often last only for a
timeless moment, a reality is experienced that exposes a gleam
of the transcendental reality, in which universe and self, sender
and receiver, are one. [The relationship of spontaneous to drug
induced enlightenment has been most extensively investigated by
R. C. Zaehner, *Mysticism: Sacred and Profane* (The Clarendon Press,
Oxford, 1957).]

Gottfried Benn, in his essay "Provoziertes Leben" [Provoked
life] (in Ausdnckswelt, Limes Verlag, Wiesbaden, 1949),
characterized the reality in which self and world are separated as
"the schizoid catastrophe, the Western entelechy neurosis." He
further writes:

> ...In the southern part of our continent this concept
> of reality began to be formed. The Hellenistic-European
> agonistic principle of victory through effort, cunning,

*malice, talent, force, and later, European Darwinism and
"superman," was instrumental in its formation. The ego
emerged, dominated, fought; for this it needed instruments,
material, power. It had a different relationship to matter,
more removed sensually, but closer formally. It analyzed
matter, tested, sorted: weapons, object of exchange, ransom
money. It clarified matter through isolation, reduced it
to formulas, took pieces out of it, divided it up. [Matter
became] a concept which hung like a disaster over the
West, with which the West fought, without grasping it,
to which it sacrified enormous quantities of blood and
happiness; a concept whose inner tension and fragmentations
it was impossible to dissolve through a natural viewing
or methodical insight into the inherent unity and peace of
prelogical forms of being... instead the cataclysmic character
of this idea became clearer and clearer... a state, a social
organization, a public morality, for which life is economically
usable life and which does not recognize the world of
provoked life, cannot stop its destructive force. A society,
whose hygiene and race cultivation as a modern ritual
is founded solely on hollow biological statistics, can only
represent the external viewpoint of the mass; for this point
of view it can wage war, incessantly, for reality is simply
raw material, but its metaphysical background remains
forever obscured. [This excerpt from Benn's essay was taken
from Ralph Metzner's translation "Provoked Life: An Essay
on the Anthropology of the Ego," which was published
in* PSYCHEDELIC REVIEW I *(1): 47-54, 1963. Minor
corrections in Metzner's text have been made by A. H.]*

As Gottfried Benn formulates it in these sentences, a concept of
reality that separates self and the world has decisively determined
the evolutionary course of European intellectual history.
Experience of the world as matter, as object, to which man stands
opposed, has produced modern natural science and technology—

creations of the Western mind that have changed the world. With their help human beings have subdued the world. Its wealth has been exploited in a manner that may be characterized as plundering, and the sublime accomplishment of technological civilization, the comfort of Western industrial society, stands face-to-face with a catastrophic destruction of the environment. Even to the heart of matter, to the nucleus of the atom and its splitting, this objective intellect has progressed and has unleashed energies that threaten all life on our planet.

A misuse of knowledge and understanding, the products of searching intelligence, could not have emerged from a consciousness of reality in which human beings are not separated from the environment but rather exist as part of living nature and the universe. All attempts today to make amends for the damage through environmentally protective measures must remain only hopeless, superficial patchwork, if no curing of the "Western entelechy neurosis" ensues, as Benn has characterized the objective reality conception. Healing would mean existential experience of a deeper, self-encompassing reality.

The experience of such a comprehensive reality is impeded in an environment rendered dead by human hands, such as is present in our great cities and industrial districts. Here the contrast between self and outer world becomes especially evident. Sensations of alienation, of loneliness, and of menace arise. It is these sensations that impress themselves on everyday consciousness in Western industrial society; they also take the upper hand everywhere that technological civilization extends itself, and they largely determine the production of modern art and literature.

There is less danger of a cleft reality experience arising in a natural environment. In field and forest, and in the animal world sheltered therein, indeed in every garden, a reality is perceptible that is infinitely more real, older, deeper, and more wondrous than everything made by people, and that will yet endure, when the inanimate, mechanical, and concrete world again vanishes, becomes rusted and fallen into ruin. In the sprouting, growth, blooming, fruiting, death, and regermination of plants, in their relationship with the sun, whose light they are able to convert into chemically bound energy in the form of organic compounds, out of which all that lives on our earth is built; in the being of plants the same mysterious, inexhaustible, eternal life energy is evident that has also brought us forth and takes us back again into its womb, and in which we are sheltered and united with all living things.

We are not leading up to a sentimental enthusiasm for nature, to "back to nature" in Rousseau's sense. That romantic movement, which sought the idyll in nature, can also be explained by a feeling of humankind's separation from nature. What is needed today is a fundamental re-experience of the oneness of all living things, a comprehensive reality consciousness that ever more infrequently develops spontaneously, the more the primordial flora and fauna of our mother earth must yield to a dead technological environment.

MYSTERY AND MYTH

The notion of reality as the self juxtaposed to the world, in confrontation with the outer world, began to form itself, as reported in the citation from Benn, in the southern portion of the European continent in Greek antiquity. No doubt people at that time knew the suffering that was connected with such a cleft reality consciousness. The Greek genius tried the cure, by supplementing the multiformed and richly colored, sensual as well as deeply sorrowful Apollonian worldview created by the subject/object cleavage, with the Dionysian world of experience, in which this cleavage is abolished in ecstatic inebriation. Nietzsche writes in *The Birth of Tragedy*:

> It is either through the influence of narcotic potions, of
> which all primitive peoples and races speak in hymns, or

*through the powerful approach of spring, penetrating with
joy all of nature, that those Dionysian stirrings arise, which
in their intensification lead the individual to forget himself
completely... Not only does the bond between man and man
come to be forged once again by the magic of the Dionysian
rite, but alienated, hostile, or subjugated nature again
celebrates her reconciliation with her prodigal son, man.*

The Mysteries of Eleusis, which were celebrated annually
in the fall, over an interval of approximately 2,000 years, from
about 1500 B.C. until the fourth century A.D., were intimately
connected with the ceremonies and festivals in honor of the god
Dionysus. These Mysteries were established by the goddess of
agriculture, Demeter, as thanks for the recovery of her daughter
Persephone, whom Hades, the god of the underworld, had
abducted. A further thank offering was the ear of grain, which
was presented by the two goddesses to Triptolemus, the first high
priest of Eleusis. They taught him the cultivation of grain, which
Triptolemus then disseminated over the whole globe. Persephone,
however, was not always allowed to remain with her mother,
because she had taken nourishment from Hades, contrary to the
order of the highest gods. As punishment she had to return to
the underworld for a part of the year. During this time, it was
winter on the earth, the plants died and were withdrawn into the
ground, to awaken to new life early in the year with Persephone's
journey to earth.

The myth of Demeter, Persephone, Hades, and the other gods,
which was enacted as a drama, formed, however, only the external
framework of events. The climax of the yearly ceremonies, which
began with a procession from Athens to Eleusis lasting several
days, was the concluding ceremony with the initiation, which
took place in the night. The initiates were forbidden by penalty of
death to divulge what they had learned, beheld, in the innermost,
holiest chamber of the temple, the *tetesterion* (goal). Not one of
the multitude that were initiated into the secret of Eleusis has

ever done this. Pausanias, Plato, many Roman emperors like Hadrian and Marcus Aurelius, and many other known personages of antiquity were party to this initiation. It must have been an illumination, a visionary glimpse of a deeper reality, an insight into the true basis of the universe. That can be concluded from the statements of initiates about the value, about the importance of the vision. Thus it is reported in a Homeric Hymn: "Blissful is he among men on Earth, who has beheld that! He who has not been initiated into the holy Mysteries, who has had no part therein, remains a corpse in gloomy darkness." Pindar speaks of the Eleusinian benediction with the following words: "Blissful is he, who after having beheld this enters on the way beneath the Earth. He knows the end of life as well as its divinely granted beginning." Cicero, also a famous initiate, likewise put in first position the splendor that fell upon his life from Eleusis, when he said: "Not only have we received the reason there, that we may live in joy, but also, besides, that we may die with better hope."

How could the mythological representation of such an obvious occurrence, which runs its course annually before our eyes—the seed grain that is dropped into the earth, dies there, in order to allow a new plant, new life, to ascend into the light—prove to be such a deep, comforting experience as that attested by the cited reports? It is traditional knowledge that the initiates were furnished with a potion, the *kykeon*, for the final ceremony. It is also known that barley extract and mint were ingredients of the kykeon. Religious scholars and scholars of mythology, like Karl Kerenyi, from whose book on the Eleusinian Mysteries (Rhein-Verlag, Zurich, 1962) the preceding statements were taken, and with whom I was associated in relation to the research on this mysterious potion [In the English publication of Kerenyi's book *Eleusis* (Schocken Books, New York, 1977) a reference is made to this collaboration.], are of the opinion that the kykeon was mixed with an hallucinogenic drug. [In *The Road to Eleusis* by R. Gordon Wasson, Albert Hofmann, and Carl A. P. Ruck (Harcourt Brace

Jovanovich, New York, 1978) the possibility is discussed that
the kykeon could have acted through an LSD-like preparation of
ergot.] That would make understandable the ecstatic-visionary
experience of the Demeter-Persephone myth, as a symbol of the
cycle of life and death in both a comprehensive and timeless
reality.

When the Gothic king Alarich, coming from the north,
invaded Greece in 396 A.D. and destroyed the sanctuary of
Eleusis, it was not only the end of a religious center, but it also
signified the decisive downfall of the ancient world. With the
monks that accompanied Alarich, Christianity penetrated into the
country that must be regarded as the cradle of European culture.

The cultural-historical meaning of the Eleusinian Mysteries,
their influence on European intellectual history, can scarcely be
overestimated. Here suffering humankind found a cure for its
rational, objective, cleft intellect, in a mystical totality experience,
that let it believe in immortality, in an everlasting existence.

This belief had survived in early Christianity, although with
other symbols. It is found as a promise, even in particular passages
of the Gospels, most clearly in the Gospel according to John, as in
Chapter 14: 120. Jesus speaks to his disciples, as he takes leave of
them:

> And I will pray the Father, and he shall give you another
> Comforter, that he may abide with you forever;
> Even the Spirit of truth; whom the world cannot receive,
> because it seeth him not, neither knoweth him: but ye know
> him; for he dwelleth with you, and shall be in you.
> I will not leave you comfortless: I will come to you. Yet a
> little while, and the world seeth me no more; but ye see me:
> because I live, ye shall live also.
> At that day ye shall know that I am in my Father, and ye
> in me, and I in you.

This promise constitutes the heart of my Christian beliefs
and my call to natural-scientific research: we will attain to

knowledge of the universe through the spirit of truth, and thereby to understanding of our being one with the deepest, most comprehensive reality, God.

Ecclesiastical Christianity, determined by the duality of creator and creation, has, however, with its nature-alienated religiosity largely obliterated the Eleusinian-Dionysian legacy of antiquity. In the Christian sphere of belief, only special blessed men have attested to a timeless, comforting reality, experienced in a spontaneous vision, an experience to which in antiquity the elite of innumerable generations had access through the initiation at Eleusis. The unio mystica of Catholic saints and the visions that the representatives of Christian mysticism—Jakob Boehme, Meister Eckhart, Angelus Silesius, Thomas Traherne, William Blake, and others—describe in their writings are obviously essentially related to the enlightenment that the initiates to the Eleusinian Mysteries experienced.

The fundamental importance of a mystical experience, for the recovery of people in Western industrial societies who are sickened by a one-sided, rational, materialistic worldview, is today given primary emphasis, not only by adherents to Eastern religious movements like Zen Buddhism, but also by leading representatives of academic psychiatry. Of the appropriate literature, we will here refer only to the books of Balthasar Staehelin, the Basel psychiatrist working in Zurich. [*Haben und Sein* (1969), *Die Welt als Du* (1970), *Urvertrauen und zweite Wirklichkeit* (1973), and *Der flnale Mensch* (1976); all published by Theologischer Verlag, Zurich.] They make reference to numerous other authors who deal with the same problem. Today a type of "metamedicine," "metapsychology," and "metapsychiatry" is beginning to call upon the metaphysical element in people, which manifests itself as an experience of a deeper, duality-surmounting reality, and to make this element a basic healing principle in therapeutic practice.

In addition, it is most significant that not only medicine

but also wider circles of our society consider the overcoming
of the dualistic, cleft worldview to be a prerequisite and basis
for the recovery and spiritual renewal of occidental civilization
and culture. This renewal could lead to the renunciation of the
materialistic philosophy of life and the development of a new
reality consciousness.

As a path to the perception of a deeper, comprehensive reality,
in which the experiencing individual is also sheltered, meditation,
in its different forms, occupies a prominent place today. The
essential difference between meditation and prayer in the usual
sense, which is based upon the duality of creator-creation, is that
meditation aspires to the abolishment of the I-you-barrier by a
fusing of object and subject, of sender and receiver, of objective
reality and self.

Objective reality, the worldview produced by the spirit of
scientific inquiry, is the myth of our time. It has replaced the
ecclesiastical-Christian and mythical-Apollonian worldview.

But this ever broadening factual knowledge, which constitutes
objective reality, need not be a desecration. On the contrary, if it
only advances deep enough, it inevitably leads to the inexplicable,
primal ground of the universe: the wonder, the mystery of the
divine— in the microcosm of the atom, in the macrocosm of
the spiral nebula, in the seeds of plants, in the body and soul of
people.

Meditation begins at the limits of objective reality, at the
farthest point yet reached by rational knowledge and perception.
Meditation thus does not mean rejection of objective reality; on
the contrary, it consists of a penetration to deeper dimensions
of reality. It is not escape into an imaginary dream world; rather
it seeks after the comprehensive truth of objective reality, by
simultaneous, stereoscopic contemplation of its surfaces and
depths.

It could become of fundamental importance, and be not merely
a transient fashion of the present, if more and more people today

would make a daily habit of devoting an hour, or at least a few minutes, to meditation. As a result of the meditative penetration and broadening of the natural-scientific worldview, a new, deepened reality consciousness would have to evolve, which would increasingly become the property of all humankind. This could become the basis of a new religiosity, which would not be based on belief in the dogmas of various religions, but rather on perception through the "spirit of truth." What is meant here is a perception, a reading and understanding of the text at first hand, "out of the book that God's finger has written" (Paracelsus), out of the creation.

The transformation of the objective worldview into a deepened and thereby religious reality consciousness can be accomplished gradually, by continuing practice of meditation. It can also come about, however, as a sudden enlightenment, a visionary experience. It is then particularly profound, blessed, and meaningful. Such a mystical experience may nevertheless "not be induced even by decade-long meditation," as Balthasar Staehelin writes. Also, it does not happen to everyone, although the capacity for mystical experience belongs to the essence of human spirituality.

Nevertheless, at Eleusis, the mystical vision, the healing, comforting experience, could be arranged in the prescribed place at the appointed time, for all of the multitudes who were initiated into the holy Mysteries. This could be accounted for by the fact that a hallucinogenic drug came into use; this, as already mentioned, is something that religious scholars believe.

The characteristic property of hallucinogens, to suspend the boundaries between the experiencing self and the outer world in an ecstatic, emotional experience, makes it possible with their help, and after suitable internal and external preparation, as it was accomplished in a perfect way at Eleusis, to evoke a mystical experience according to plan, so to speak.

Meditation is a preparation for the same goal that was aspired to and was attained in the Eleusinian Mysteries. Accordingly it seems feasible that in the future, with the help of LSD, the mystical vision, crowning meditation, could be made accessible to an increasing number of practitioners of meditation.

I SEE THE TRUE IMPORTANCE OF LSD in the possibitity of providing material aid to meditation aimed at the mystical experience of a deeper, comprehensive reality. Such a use accords entirely with the essence and working character of LSD as a sacred drug.

Appendix: The Digital Hofmann Collection

BEFORE WIDESPREAD RECREATIONAL USE and media hysteria brought psychedelic research to a halt, LSD and psilocybin were the subjects of thousands of studies worldwide, conducted with the full support of academic institutions and governments. This "golden age" of psychedelic research is documented in the Hofmann Collection, a free online database of peer-reviewed, scientific journal articles on LSD and psilocybin.

Originally compiled by the staff of the Sandoz Pharmaceutical Corporation during Albert Hofmann's residence there, the collection represents nearly every research paper on LSD or psilocybin published between the mid-1940s and the mid-1970s. The papers reflect the evolving trends in psychiatry and culture over the decades, and changing perceptions of psychedelics' risks and benefits. About 80% of the articles are published in English, and 20% are in other languages.

The project to digitize the papers has been a joint effort of MAPS (the Multidisciplinary Association for Psychedelic Studies), the Albert Hofmann Foundation, Erowid (a comprehensive drug information website, www.erowid.org), the Promind Foundation, and the Heffter Research Institute. In 1996, Sandoz donated the collection to the Albert Hofmann Foundation, and the papers were displayed in the AHF Museum in Los Angeles while funding lasted. Beginning the process of making the papers accessible, the AHF collaborated with MAPS and Heffter to create a digital index of the nearly 4,000 papers.

In 2001, this work was taken up by the Erowid team, who first verified and completed the index. With support from MAPS and the Promind Foundation, each paper was then scanned, converted to PDF format, and linked to its index entry in an online database. The original articles were moved to archival-quality sleeves and placed in sequential binders. After the completion of the project in 2002, the entire collection, about 30 large boxes, was returned to Switzerland for eventual installment in a new library.

The articles in the Hofmann Collection are available online for downloading or printing; searches are by author, title, journal, abstract, or year. Many of the English-language papers are fully text-searchable, though in cases where the source itself was a poor photocopy or otherwise damaged, this was not possible. In a few hundred entries the article is simply missing, but in most cases there is at least a link to the paper's abstract. Most of the missing papers probably exist in libraries or university collections somewhere in the world, and those who come across them are encouraged to send them in for posting.

With the digitizing of the Hofmann Collection, the wealth of the world's scientific literature on LSD and psilocybin is now accessible and permanently available. It is hoped that this resource will help to inform the discussion on psychedelics and aid future researchers who seek permission to study their risks and benefits.

HOW TO ACCESS THE HOFMANN COLLECTION:

You can search the Hofmann Collection online in one of two ways:

http://www.maps.org/wwwpb/

The Psychedelic Bibliography, which includes several other databases of psychedelic research, including the MAPS MDMA Literature Review project, which is updated monthly with PDFs of new papers on MDMA.

Or

http://www.erowid.org/references/hofmann_collection.php

The Erowid Hofmann Collection page offers a number of links with information about the collection's contents, its history, and how it is organized. Related databases are available at http://www.erowid.org/references/ in a very easy-to-use format.

LSD: My Problem Child Index

INDEX

Ska Maria Pastora 139–155
  botanical identification 145,153
  investigation of psychoactive component 154
  religious use 145–148,150–152
Spiritual potential of psychedelics 31–32,180,186–189,192–193,197–210. *See also* Mystical experience; *See also* Mushrooms, psilocybin: religious use
Spofa pharmaceutical firm 191
Stadler, Paul A. 60
Staehelin, Balthasar 206,208
Stoll, Arthur 35–37,41–42,84
Stoll, Werner A. 63–70

T
Teonanacatl 119. *See also* Mushrooms, psilocybin
Troxler, Franz 59,61,128
Tscherter, Hans 125,135
Turbina corymbosa. *See* Ololiuhqui

V
Vogt, Walter 25,183–189
Von Bibra, Ernst Freiherrn 162

W
Wasson, R. Gordon 118,120,121,123–124,132,134,139–155,186
  first mushroom ceremony 124
Wasson, Valentina Pavlovna 118,121,123
Weitlaner, Robert J. 121,140
Willstatter, Richard 42

About the Publisher

Founded in 1986, the Multidisciplinary Association for Psychedelic Studies (MAPS) is a membership-based, IRS-approved 501 (c) (3) non-profit research and educational organization. We assist scientists to design, fund, obtain approval for, conduct, and report on studies evaluating the risks and benefits of MDMA, psychedelic drugs, and marijuana. MAPS' mission is to sponsor scientific research designed to develop psychedelics and marijuana into FDA-approved prescription medicines and to educate the public honestly about the risks and benefits of these drugs.

For decades, the government was the biggest obstacle to research. Now that long-awaited research is finally being approved, the formidable challenge is funding it. At present, there is no funding available from governments, pharmaceutical companies, or major foundations. That means, for the time being, the future of psychedelic and marijuana research rests in the hands of people like you.

Can you imagine a cultural reintegration of the use of psychedelics and the states of mind they engender? Please join MAPS in supporting the expansion of scientific knowledge in this promising area. Progress is only possible with the support of individuals who care enough to take individual and collective action.

How MAPS Has Made a Difference

- Sponsored and obtained approval for the first LSD-assisted psychotherapy study in over 35 years. The study is taking place in Switzerland in subjects with anxiety associated with end-of-life issues.
- Sponsored the first US FDA-approved study evaluating MDMA's therapeutic applications, for subjects with chronic post-traumatic stress disorder (PTSD), as well as MDMA/PTSD pilot studies in Switzerland, Israel and Spain.
- Waged a successful lawsuit against DEA in support of Professor Lyle Craker's proposed MAPS-sponsored medical marijuana production facility at the University of Massachusetts-Amherst; led campaigns to gain support from over 50 members of the US House of Representatives.
- Supported long-term follow-up studies of pioneering research with LSD and psilocybin from the 1950s and 1960s.
- Sponsored Dr. Evgeny Krupitsky's pioneering research into the use of ketamine- assisted psychotherapy in the treatment of alcoholism and heroin addiction.
- Assisted Dr. Charles Grob to obtain permission for the first human studies in the United States with MDMA after it was criminalized in 1985.
- Sponsored the first study to analyze the purity and potency of street samples of "Ecstasy" and medical marijuana.
- Funded the successful effort of Dr. Donald Abrams to obtain permission for the first human study into the therapeutic use of marijuana in 15 years, and to secure a $1-million grant from the National Institute on Drug Abuse.
- Obtained orphan-drug designation from the FDA for smoked marijuana in the treatment of AIDS Wasting Syndrome.
- Funded the synthesis of psilocybin for the first FDA-approved study in a patient population in twenty-five years.
- Sponsored "Psychedelic Peer Support" programs and services at events, concerts, schools, and churches.

Why Give?

For more information or to join our online mailing list, please visit
maps.org/donate.

Your donation will help create a world where psychedelics and marijuana are available by prescription for medical uses, and where they can safely and legally be used for personal growth, creativity, and spirituality.

Every dollar we spend on this work has come from visionary individuals committed to our mission. For-profit drug companies don't invest because there is no economic incentive to develop these drugs; these compounds cannot be patented and are taken only a few times. We're encouraging government agencies and major public foundations to support our research. For now, however, it's up to individuals like you to support the future of psychedelic medicine.

Donations are tax-deductible as allowed by law, and may be made by credit card or personal check (made out to MAPS). Gifts of stock are also welcome, and we encourage supporters to include MAPS in their will or estate plans.

MAPS takes your privacy seriously. The MAPS email list is strictly confidential and will not be shared with other organizations. The *MAPS Bulletin* is mailed in a plain white envelope.

Sign up for our monthly email newsletter at **maps.org**.

MAPS
1115 Mission St., Santa Cruz, CA 95060 USA
Phone: 831-429-MDMA (6362)
Fax: 831-429-6370
E-mail: askmaps@maps.org
Web: maps.org | mdmaptsd.org

More Books Published by MAPS

Available at **maps.org/store**.

Ayahuasca Religions: A Comprehensive Bibliography & Critical Essays
By Beatriz Caiuby Labate, Isabel Santana de Rose, and Rafael Guimarães
dos Santos. Translated by Matthew Meyer, 2009
ISBN: 978-0-9798622-1-2 $11.95
The last few decades have seen a broad expansion of the ayahuasca
religions, and (especially since the millennium) an explosion of studies
into the spiritual uses of ayahuasca. *Ayahuasca Religions* grew out of
the need for a catalogue of the large and growing list of titles related to
this subject, and offers a map of the global literature. Three researchers
located in different cities (Beatriz Caiuby Labate in São Paulo, Rafael
Guimarães dos Santos in Barcelona, and Isabel Santana de Rose in Flori-
anópolis, Brazil) worked in a virtual research group for a year to compile
a list of bibliographical references on Santo Daime, Barquinha, the União
do Vegetal (UDV), and urban ayahuasqueiros. The review includes spe-
cialized academic literature as well as esoteric and experiential writings
produced by participants of ayahuasca churches.

Drawing it Out
By Sherana Harriet Francis, 2001
ISBN: 0-9669919-5-8 $19.95
Artist Sherana Francis' fascinating exploration of her LSD psychotherapy
experience contains a series of 61 black-and-white illustrations along with
accompanying text. The book documents the author's journey through a
symbolic death and rebirth, with powerful surrealist self-portraits of her
psyche undergoing transformation. Francis' images unearth universal experiences of facing the unconscious as they reflect her personal struggle
towards healing. An 8.5-by-11 inch paperback with an introduction by
Stan Grof, this makes an excellent coffee table book.

Healing with Entactogens: Therapist and Patient Perspectives on MDMA-Assisted Group Psychotherapy
By Torsten Passie, M.D.; foreword by Ralph Metzner, Ph.D., 2012
ISBN: 0-9798622-7-2 $12.95
In this booklet, Torsten Passie, M.D., a leading European authority on psychedelic compound, explores MDMA and other entactogens as pharmacological adjuncts to group psychotherapy. It presents intimate insights into entactogenic experiences from first-hand accounts of clients who participated in group therapy sessions, and crucial background on the neurobiological and psychospiritual components of those experiences. The word "entactogen" refers to compounds that "produce a touching within," and is derived from the roots *en* (Greek: within), *tact's* (Latin: touch), and *gen* (Greek: produce. Entactogen is used to describe a class of psychoactive substances that decrease anxiety; increase trust, self-acceptance, and openness; and allow easier access to memories, providing fertile ground for transformative healing.

Honor Thy Daughter
By Marilyn Howell, Ed.D., 2011
ISBN: 0-9798622-6-4 $16.95
This is an intimate true story by Marilyn Howell, Ed.D., about her family's search for physical, emotional, and spiritual healing as her daughter struggles with terminal cancer. The family's journey takes them through the darkest corners of corporate medicine, the jungles of Brazil, the pallid hallways of countless hospitals, and ultimately into the hands of an anonymous therapist who offers the family hope and healing through MDMA-assisted psychotherapy. The story was originally featured in a 2006 Boston Globe article entitled "A Good Death" in which Howell's identity was concealed. With psychedelic medicine increasingly a part of the mainstream vocabulary, in this poignant new book Howell comes out of the closet and shares with us how psychedelic therapy helped heal the bonds ripped apart by illness.

Ketamine: Dreams and Realities
By Karl Jansen, M.D., Ph.D., 2004
ISBN: 0-9660019-7-4 $14.95
London researcher Dr. Karl Jansen has studied ketamine at every level, from photographing the receptors to which ketamine binds in the human brain to observing the similarities between the psychoactive effects of the drug and near-death experiences. He writes about ketamine's potential as an adjunct to psychotherapy, as well as about its addictive nature and methods of treating addiction. Jansen is the world's foremost expert on ketamine, and this is a great resource for anyone who wishes to understand ketamine's effects, risks, and potential.

LSD: My Problem Child
By Albert Hofmann, Ph.D. (4th English edition, paperback), 2009
ISBN: 978-0-9798622-2-9 $15.95
This is the story of LSD told by a concerned yet hopeful father. Organic chemist Albert Hofmann traces LSD's path from a promising psychiatric research medicine to a recreational drug sparking hysteria and prohibition. We follow Hofmann's trek across Mexico to discover sacred plants related to LSD and listen as he corresponds with other notable figures about his remarkable discovery. Underlying it all is Dr. Hofmann's powerful conclusion that mystical experience may be our planet's best hope for survival. Whether induced by LSD, meditation, or arising spontaneously, such experiences help us to comprehend "the wonder, the mystery of the divine in the microcosm of the atom, in the macrocosm of the spiral nebula, in the seeds of plants, in the body and soul of people." More than sixty years after the birth of Albert Hofmann's "problem child," his vision of its true potential is more relevant—and more needed—than ever. The eulogy that Dr. Hofmann wrote himself and was read by his children at his funeral is the forward to the 4th edition.

LSD Psychotherapy
By Stanislav Grof, M.D. (4th Edition, Paperback), 2008
ISBN: 0-9798622-0-5 $19.95
LSD Psychotherapy is a complete study of the use of LSD in clinical therapeutic practice, written by the world's foremost LSD psychotherapist. The text was written as a medical manual and as a historical record portraying a broad therapeutic vision. It is a valuable source of information for anyone wishing to learn more about LSD. The therapeutic model also extends to other substances: the MAPS research team used *LSD Psychotherapy* as a key reference for its first MDMA/PTSD study. Originally published in 1980, this 2008 paperback edition has a new introduction by Albert Hofmann, Ph.D., a forward by Andrew Weil, M.D., and color illustrations.

The Secret Chief Revealed
By Myron Stolaroff, 2005
ISBN: 0-9669919-6-6 $12.95
The second edition of *The Secret Chief* is a collection of interviews with "Jacob," the underground psychedelic therapist who is revealed years after his death as psychologist Leo Zeff. Before his death in 1988, Zeff provided psychedelic therapy to over 3,000 people. As "Jacob," he relates the origins of his early interest in psychedelics, how he chose his clients, and what he did to prepare them. He discusses the dynamics of the individual and group trip, the characteristics and appropriate dosages of various drugs, and the range of problems that people worked through. Stanislav Grof, Ann and Alexander Shulgin, and Albert Hofmann each contribute writings about the importance of Leo's work. In this new edition, Leo's family and former clients also write about their experiences with him. This book is an easy-to-read introduction to the techniques and potential of psychedelic therapy.

The Ultimate Journey: Consciousness and the Mystery of Death
By Stanislav Grof, M.D., Ph.D. (2nd edition), 2006
ISBN: 0-9660019-9-0 $19.95
Dr. Stanislav Grof, author of *LSD Psychotherapy* and originator of Holotropic Breathwork, offers a wealth of perspectives on how we can enrich and transform the experience of dying in our culture. This 356-page book features 40 pages of images (24 in color) and a foreword by Huston Smith. Grof discusses his own patients' experiences of death and rebirth in psychedelic therapy, investigates cross-cultural beliefs and paranormal and near-death research, and argues that contrary to the predominant Western perspective death is not necessarily the end of consciousness. Grof is a psychiatrist with over forty years of experience with research into non-ordinary states of consciousness and one of the founders of transpersonal psychology. He is the founder of the International Transpersonal Association, and has published over 140 articles in professional journals. The latest edition of *The Ultimate Journey* includes a new foreword by David Jay Brown, M.A., and Peter Gasser, M.D.

Shipping and Handling

MAPS
1115 Mission St., Santa Cruz, CA 95060 USA
Phone: 831-429-MDMA (6362), Fax: 831-429-6370
E-mail: orders@maps.org, Web: maps.org/store